Safe at Home

Safe at Home

FINDING WHAT YOU NEVER LOST

To Linda, Derek, Sage and Jameson—
Dear friends—
Much love

Stephen D. McConnell

ISBN: 1514712717
ISBN 13: 9781514712719
Library of Congress Control Number: 2015910418
CreateSpace Independent Publishing Platform,
North Charleston, South Carolina

To Job's Friends
Proverbs 18:24

Contents

The Gospel According to Baseball

Preface

WHEN I WAS YOUNG I had one of those great boyhood days of playing with my buddies. We started in the morning outside playing any kind of sport we could think of. We moved from that to riding our bikes for a while, and then from there to swimming at the public pool. The day ended with a game of hide-and-seek. It was raining by then, so we took the game indoors, and since it was my house I had the clear advantage. I went to my perfect place to hide—a closet that was hard to find. I laid down on the floor and waited. I waited. I waited. The next thing I knew I was opening my eyes. *Am I still waiting? And why am I in my bed? How can I be in my bed when I was in the closet?* It took awhile to put the pieces together. My perfect hiding place had not only stumped my friends but also doubled for the perfect place to fall asleep. My exhausting day came to an end, unbeknownst to me, in a nap. And since my mother knew my favorite hiding place, she found me asleep. She sent the boys home and asked my father to deliver me to bed—all without my knowing it. I went from the pride of a perfect hiding place to being found and delivered safely to my bed without any awareness. Strange what can be happening around you and to you without your knowing it.

Luke the Gospel writer tells us a story of a strange thing that happens after the women and the disciples discover Jesus' tomb empty. Two men are walking to a town called Emmaus and talking about the sad events of Jesus' death, and suddenly another man joins them—a stranger who does not seem clued in to what has happened to Jesus in Jerusalem. But they welcome the man into their conversation completely unaware that the resurrected Jesus is walking with them. Something is happening around them and to them without their knowing it. When they arrive at their destination they implore the stranger to join them for a meal and for the night. At table, Luke tells us, the stranger "took bread, blessed it, broke it, and gave it to them." It's the same thing Jesus did to feed the five thousand. It's the same thing Jesus did to feed the disciples at the Last Supper—he took bread, blessed it, broke it, and gave it. And Luke tells us that when he did this for these travelers, their eyes were opened and they recognized him. Until then, though, much had happened that they had not seen.

One of the great discoveries in the world of the Spirit is the realization of how much has happened, and how much is happening, without our knowing. How can two followers of Jesus not recognize him while walking miles with him? How can Mary Magdalene find Jesus outside the tomb and think he's the gardener? How can the resurrected Jesus gather his disciples on a mountain, yet some still doubt? How can the fishermen disciples see Jesus on the shore cooking bread and fish (hint: loaves and fish and five thousand) and still not know it's Jesus? It's because we're in the world of the Spirit. And what the world of the Spirit has to teach us is that God is mysteriously already ahead of us, behind us, and beside us—and that as uncertain as this world is, the one thing we can count on is the One who never lets us go. "I am convinced," wrote the apostle Paul, "that neither death nor life, nor angels, nor rulers, nor things present, nor things to come, nor powers, nor height, nor depth, nor anything else in all creation will be able to separate us from the love of God in Christ Jesus our Lord."

We don't have to see it to be true. We don't have to know it to be true. We don't have to recognize it to be true. It's just true. And as sure as I laid in my father's arms as he walked me up the stairs to bed—without any clue on my part—so true it is that this resurrected Jesus dwells in our midst and walks by our side while we run about hiding and seeking.

How might our lives be different if we awoke each day with a deep and abiding sense that the God of the universe is as present and as real as the hearts that beat inside our chests? That this loving God who created us has already gone ahead of us? That as we grab our keys and rush out the door for another day oblivious to the presence of God, still this loving God in Christ Jesus will walk with us and never let us go?

Christ's presence doesn't mean that the path and journey are safe. They're not. And God is not some kind of force field protecting us. Bad things happen that can keep us from a safe arrival to our earthly destinations. Each of us can recite our own stories or those of folks we know when a safe arrival didn't happen. There are no guaranteed journeys in this life, but in the words of the Psalmist, "He will keep your going out and your coming in from this time forth and forevermore."

Life can take on a whole new meaning if we can abide in this good news—that God will always keep us, that nothing separates us from the love of God and nothing can keep us from the abiding home of his presence. If we can hold onto that, just think how adventurous and courageous life can be. We might play for different stakes if we knew that God's love and God's promise were never in doubt.

I hope and pray that the following pages will be an encouragement to you. Some chapters will comfort, some will challenge. And in the end I leave you with the Gospel According to Baseball—that great national pastime that begins at home and ends at home. And though the in-between is filled with strikes and balls and outs and steals and sacrifices and errors, what never changes is the fact that we begin at home and we end at home. Safely. May that promise inspire you to step up to the plate and take your turn at bat.

CHAPTER 1

The Moment

—✥—

Matthew 25:1–13

PERHAPS ONE OF THE GREATEST moments in U.S. Olympic history took place in Atlanta in 1996 when the US women's gymnastics team took the team competition down to the wire against the Russians. Only tenths of a point separated the two teams and it boiled down to the performance of an eighteen-year-old American woman—Kerri Strug—and her performance on the vault. Most of us remember this. One good run, one good flip, one good landing is what it would take to give the Americans their first Olympic gold medal in the women's gymnastics team competition. The first of Kerri's two attempts resulted in a poor landing in which she injured her ankle: a sprain and torn tendons—a significant injury that would keep most of us off our feet. Visibly limping she winced her way back to the start of the runway to prepare for her second vault. A poor run, a poor jump, a poor landing, and the Americans might lose. And there she stood with the world looking on. It was, for her, *the moment.*

Rewind fifteen years to when Kerri was three years old and with an older sister who was already a competing gymnast: Kerri began training. Three years old. Fifteen years of training. Moving from gym to gym, town to town, coach to coach. Injuries, medals, emotional breakdowns, training, training, training. Every day of every week of every year had brought her to this point, where she stood before the world with an injured ankle, expected to run and spin and spring and land on her two feet perfectly. It was the moment her whole life had been about. Everything had been preparation for this time. And she was ready—and she did it. Team USA took the gold, and Kerri appeared on the Wheaties box.

Four days later a security guard, Richard Jewell, working the overnight detail at Centennial Park in Atlanta, noticed a backpack sitting unattended under a park bench. It was the moment. Likely one of a hundred left-behind backpacks amid the millions of Olympic visitors—why bother? But Richard Jewell bothered and took the chance to inconvenience hundreds of people by spending the next several minutes clearing the area, escorting hundreds to a perimeter of safety at the risk of being labeled an alarmist. Thirteen minutes later the backpack exploded, and while many were hurt and one was killed, clearly Richard Jewell had saved scores if not hundreds. It was *the moment.* Unfortunately, Richard Jewell did not end up on a Wheaties box. He ended up being tried unjustly in the newspapers and television—suspected of having planted the bomb in order to play hero. The next months were the worst of his life, as America scorned him and made fun of him. It took ten years for the US Attorney's Office to formally clear him of all charges. Americans reluctantly and belatedly praised him. He died the following year.

Who's to know when the moment will come and what will happen once it comes? Rare, of course, is any particular life that ends up before millions of sports viewers, or before an explosive device, when all hangs in the balance. Will she stick the landing? Will he protect the crowd? Most of us have never found ourselves in such moments of high spectator drama. And with that in mind, perhaps it is tempting for you and me to imagine that maybe what we do from day to day in the grand scheme doesn't much matter. Since we're not aiming for a gold medal and since the chances of diffusing a terrorist plot are slim, what's the big difference with what I do every day? What's the point of preparing if the high drama is likely never to come?

Perhaps it's the question Jesus is trying to answer in the parables that Matthew shares with us in chapter 25 of his Gospel—in particular the story of the wise and the foolish maidens waiting for the wedding. Borrowing from the customs of a first-century Palestinian wedding, Jesus wonders if the kingdom of heaven isn't a little like waiting for the moment when the bridegroom starts the parade into the wedding feast accompanied by the bridesmaids, all with lamps aflame. One does not know when the moment will come, when the bridegroom will arrive. Matthew is writing his Gospel for a crowd of people who have every expectation that the Messiah will return imminently—certainly within their lifetime—but he appears delayed. But the kingdom could come at any time; the Christ could arrive at any moment. And when that moment comes, will you be ready? And since we don't know when that moment will come, what we realize is that life isn't about fixating on that promised moment ahead as much as about focusing on the present moment, for it is in the moment at hand that Jesus promised his presence. Right? We are practicing the presence of the Messiah every day. Jesus said, "The kingdom of heaven is . . . what? Is at hand. Is in your midst. Is within you." So every moment is the practice of the presence of Christ.

And we practice the presence of Christ for those moments that happen to us daily in which we become bearers of the light. Daily we are being called to have on hand the oil that fuels the fire that brings the light into the world—that we might let our light shine so that others might see our good works and give glory to our Father in heaven. The moment doesn't happen when the camera crews are rolling and when the angels are descending. The moment comes in every moment in which we have the chance to practice the presence of Christ and to find the presence of Christ in every human being who should come our way.

We prepare for Jesus' triumphant coming in the future in every single person who comes to us now. Every moment is preparation for *the* moment.

I do my fair share of airplane traveling; many of us do. And there comes a point when flying on a plane gets to feel a little routine. You get on a plane, sit down, buckle your seat belt, listen to the attendant run through the instructions, taxi to the end of the runway—and then comes that moment when the pilot opens the throttle and the engines thrust and the plane starts speeding down the runway. If you fly enough, all that is routine. Even the lifting of many tons of airplane, not to mention a few hundred people, off the ground and above the clouds—all this is routine, all in a pilot's day's work. She spent years training for this moment, and we count on her. But as routine as it is, nothing erases the fact that a few hundred souls are defying gravity and flying, seemingly in spite of the laws of the universe. We don't pay a lot of attention to that, unless you are Chesley B. Sullenberger and you see a flock of geese fly into your jet engines and you know that there is no airport close enough to land your powerless plane. Then you know what every moment up until then has been for. You have to employ all those flights, all those training classes, all those flight simulator sessions, because now, like Kerri Strug, you are at the end of a runway and you have to make the landing stick. The only difference is that you have hundreds of souls in your care. These lives are hanging in the balance, and that is a river I'm trying to land on. Now, all of a sudden, every moment that has led to this moment has been inestimable in value.

In every hospital, surgeons do their work: appendix are removed, gall bladders taken, arteries bypassed, discs fused, cancers cut out—it happens thousand of times a day—and maybe there is even a bit of routine to it all. But when I sat in the holding room years ago and watched them wheel my daughter away into surgery, there was nothing routine. It was *the moment*—and it was the moment for that surgeon, as far as I was concerned—a moment that I prayed had been preceded by thousands of other moments preparing him for this moment. *This moment.*

So when Jesus tells us the story about the five wise maidens and the five foolish maidens—five prepared and five unprepared—there comes with it this invitation to a rhythm of life that finds us more and more aware and awake to the moments of Messiah in our midst. In other words we live with the arrival of Jesus every day. "I will be with you," he says, "to the close of the age." The truth is that Jesus is with us in every moment when we have the chance to shine the light—to bring peace and justice and purity of heart and righteousness and meekness and courage to a world that wonders if God really is around. This is the rhythm to which we are invited. Brother Lawrence, in his treasured book, *Practicing the Presence of God*—says it this way: "We ought not to be weary of doing little things for the love of God, who regards not the greatness of the work, but the love with which it is performed." And we do so because moment to moment we are in the presence of Christ the bridegroom.

The Celts of long ago fashioned the rhythm into the prayer of St. Patrick:

> I rise today:
> in power's strength, invoking the Trinity,
> believing in threeness,
> confessing the oneness,

of Creation's Creator.
Christ with me, Christ before me, Christ behind me;
Christ within me, Christ beneath me, Christ above me;
Christ to the right of me, Christ to the left of me;
Christ in my lying, Christ in my sitting, Christ in my
rising;
Christ in the heart of all who think of me,
Christ on the tongue of all who speak to me,
Christ in the eye of all who see me,
Christ in the ear of all who hear me.
I rise today in spirit's strength . . .
The practiced presence of Christ.

Perhaps it was such practice that prepared those good Christian souls to know what to do when the moment came. I'm thinking of the Nickel Mine, Pennsylvania, Mennonite community that fell victim to a mentally ill gunman who took the lives of five Amish girls in their schoolhouse. It was the moment. What is a Christian community to do? Well, they had been practicing for four hundred years the art of reconciliation and forgiveness. It was their tradition. Peacemaking. In just hours they assembled to pray for the families of those girls—of course—but also to pray for the family of the assailant. And to set up a fund for that family and invite them into their homes. And to raze that school building of haunting memories and build a new school—the New Hope School. They had been practicing the presence of Christ so that when Messiah came in the broken hearts of an ostracized family the community was prepared.

Sobering, such radical grace. But don't you wonder if that isn't what this weary old world is looking for? Don't you wonder if the moment is upon us—with all this radical badness in the world—that we as brothers and sisters of the bridegroom, maidens with our lamps, light the world with our radical goodness? Seeing this moment as the moment? At least use this moment to ask yourself: *What am I waiting for?* Christ shall someday come with his angels, of course. But Christ comes today, too, in those souls. Those souls within reach of my life, your life—scores, hundreds of souls—Christ on the tongue of all who speak to me, Christ in the eye of all who see me, Christ in the ear of all who hear me. Souls for whom radical goodness from you might shine the light and make the difference.

What are you waiting for? Is it possible that all your moments have been meant for this moment?

CHAPTER 2

Dress Code

—⁓—

Matthew 22:1–14; John 13:1–11

I READ AN ARTICLE A few years ago about a man named Ralph Golio, a restaurant owner up in Massachusetts who decided he wanted to offer a free lunch. Ralph had had a pretty serious heart attack that he managed to survive, and out of gratitude for being given another chance at life he made a deal with God that he would offer free lunches to any person over the age of sixty-five. Free. No charge. Come in and have your choice of roast beef and mashed potatoes or haddock with Creole sauce (not necessarily a heart-happy diet—but hey, beggars can't be choosers). Ralph put his offer in the paper, placed signs in his windows, and prepared for a line out the door. And much to his surprise, almost nobody came. A few folks who knew the wisdom of never turning down a free lunch arrived and tried it out, but for the most part Ralph learned that people thought there was a catch. No such thing as a free lunch. Must be a gimmick. No restaurant gives away food. Must be overstock he's trying to get rid of. But it's free, Ralph would insist. No, they said—there must be some kind of catch.

No such thing as a free lunch.

We live in a world, don't we, of catches? We live in a world of gimmicks, tricks to get you to sign on the dotted line. Pay more than it's worth. Bait and switch. "A sucker's born every minute" (attributed to P. T. Barnum). Someone said that when you put together the man with experience but no money with the man who has money but no experience, the man with the experience gets the money and the man with the money gets the experience. We were taught long ago to be on the watch; any offer that seems too good to be true is just that: an offer too good to be true. You only get what you pay for. Just ask Ralph Golio.

So maybe Ralph Golio would be nodding his head if he were to hear Jesus' story about the king and his feast. The king has prepared a feast for his people. He made the invitation list and is eager to eat, drink, and be merry, but maybe it's too good to be true. Maybe there's a catch. Maybe it's a gimmick. Can't be too good if you're not charging anything. So everybody has some sort of excuse to miss the feast. Maybe the word has gotten out on Facebook or Twitter that the right people don't seem to be going. The beautiful people won't be there. Better to go to one of those restaurants that require a second mortgage for portions one-tenth the size of the plate. Lord knows the reasons, and the Lord is not happy.

The heck with them, he says. Let's open the gates and invite anyone who wants to come—the good and the bad.

Doesn't matter; I'm just interested in a party. I want people who want to be here. And so they come—those who are not too smart for their own good, people who know a bargain when they see it. And they come into this kingdom of the free lunch. They eat, they drink, and they make merry. It's what the kingdom is, Jesus says. It's the free lunch. Pity those, Jesus says, who are just too smart for their own good, those people who want to be in those circles that you have to earn yourself into. Have you ever been in one of those? It happened long ago when we were young. You didn't have to get much beyond the first grade to find the circle of the smart kids, or the cool kids, or the athletic kids, or the rich kids. And maybe you or your parents spent a lot of time trying to earn you into one of those circles. Maybe you'd do anything to earn yourself into one of those circles, even sell your soul. Some of us did.

Junior high was my time. I was not particularly cool, smart, or athletic. Oh, but there was that group: cool, smart, and athletic. I worked so hard to be something I really wasn't, and guess what? I made it. I earned my way into the group, and once I arrived I realized two things: the group was not what I thought it was—they really weren't very nice people—and lo and behold, I was turning into someone who was not very nice either. Of course, it doesn't stop in childhood. The older we get, the higher the stakes. Oh, what we might do to get ourselves into the right group, the right club, the right organization, the right college, the right fraternity. What little parts of our soul are we willing to sell to earn our way in?

C. S. Lewis writes about the Inner Ring—and that one of the great temptations we all face is the temptation to get ourselves into the Inner Ring. But we give away so much to get there. Writes Lewis, "Of all passions the passion for the Inner Ring is the most skillful in making a man who is not yet a very bad man do very bad things."

So, the king says, join me for lunch. Join the group—the one you don't have to earn yourself into. The group of people who know a bargain when they see it.

I love the scene in Kurt Vonnegut's novel *Jailbird* where Walter Starbuck, a man who has been imprisoned for a couple of years for a Watergate crime, is released—and he is left to stumble around wondering if he has any value . . . any worth . . . any chance of being accepted after what he has done. He makes his way over to a coffee shop, and this is how Vonnegut describes the scene:

> By the time I reached the coffee-shop door . . . my self-confidence had collapsed. Panic had taken its place. I believed I was the ugliest, dirtiest little old bum in Manhattan. If I went into the coffee shop, everybody would be nauseated. They would throw me out and tell me to go to the Bowery where I belonged. But I somehow found the courage to go in anyway—and imagine my surprise! It was as though I had died and gone to heaven! A waitress said to me, "Honeybunch, you sit right down, and I'll bring you your coffee right away." I hadn't said anything to her. So I sit down, and

> everywhere I looked I saw customers of every description being received with love. To the waitresses everybody was "honeybunch" and "darling" and "dear." It was like an emergency ward after a great catastrophe. It did not matter what race or class the victims belonged to. They were all given the same miracle drug, which was coffee. The catastrophe in this case, of course, was that the sun had come up again.
>
> I had the feeling that if Frankenstein's monster crashed into the coffee shop through a brick wall, all anybody would say to him was, "You sit down here, Lambchop, and I'll bring you your coffee right away."

Such is the feast of the kingdom, the feast for those who know a bargain when they see it.

But then Matthew gives us a twist we don't see in the other Gospels. The story is not over. A surprise is yet to come. Once the party has started for the good, the bad, and the ugly—namely, you and me—the king looks around and notices one person who's not wearing the right outfit. There has been a violation of the dress code, and much to our surprise, the king's response is very harsh. The one who is not dressed right is thrown out.

Whoa . . . whoa . . . we say. How can this be? Isn't this the kingdom of the free lunch? Isn't this the party for the good, the bad, and the ugly, and now you're talking about a dress code? Excuse me? You see, I knew there'd be a catch. I knew it was too good to be true. Bait and switch. Fine print at the bottom of the page!

We might jump to this suspicion, we who have been taught to be on our guard, to look out for the catch, the gimmick, the come-on. But maybe there's more to it than that. Maybe because it's Matthew's Gospel—Matthew's telling of the story—we might remember that a punch line is coming soon. And the punch line indeed comes in a few more chapters when Jesus tells us that the king who has just given the free lunch will someday come with his angels to separate the sheep and the goats—and in that moment we will see what the king has been looking for: those who got the point that they in fact got a free lunch. They were the good, the bad, and the ugly—and they've been given a meal they've never earned. So struck by the fact that they've been given a free feast, they get the point: the kingdom is not just about getting the free lunch, it's about the giving of the free lunch. To the least of these—the sick, the hungry, the homeless, the imprisoned, the lonely—this is what the kingdom is about. The dress code is not what we might think. It's not the black tie, it's not the evening gown, it's not the Giorgio Armani. You'd be out of place in such attire. No, the king is looking for servants' coats. He's looking for aprons. He's looking for rolled-up sleeves. He's looking for dirty jeans. He's looking for those who see the joy of tasting the meal and then serving it.

It's what Jesus was trying to make so clear in that last feast, the one we read about in John's Gospel. That while those disciples had spent so much of their time trying to figure out who was the greatest in the kingdom, who was going to sit at the right hand and left hand of the Savior—it's Jesus who stands up before them in that last meal and shows them what the kingdom is about. It's not just in the partaking, it's in the serving. He wraps a towel around his waist, bends, and washes the feet of the good, the bad, and the ugly. Yes, there is a dress code for this meal. It's whatever you have to wear to make sure someone else gets the free meal.

It's what John Williams saw. John Williams, bus driver in Milwaukee, Wisconsin, was driving his bus on one of those bone-chilling ten-degree Wisconsin days that we've all escaped from. He pulled up at the stop to let on the next group of travelers. One was a pregnant woman with tattered coat, torn socks, and no shoes. Ten degrees, and no shoes. John looked in the mirror to see where she sat and wondered what to do. He didn't have to wonder too long, for in his mirror he watched fourteen-year-old Frank Daily walk forward from the back of the bus in his bare feet with socks and shoes in hand and said, "Try these."

Towels around your waist; sockless, shoeless feet—it's the new fashion.

Paul talked about it when he offered his list of fashion statements. Said the apostle, "Clothe yourself with compassion, kindness, humility, meekness, and patience—and above all put on love which binds every part of the outfit together."

Maybe that's what Charles Stoddard was seeing when he visited the legendary leper colony on the Molokai peninsula in Hawaii. Historic suspicions about leprosy and its contagion led twenty-plus centuries of human civilization—from before the days of Jesus—to treat lepers worse than animals and to banish them to remote places like Molokai to fend for themselves and to die on their own. A young Catholic priest, Father Damien, sensed the call to offer himself to the Molokai community to minister to the least of these. He put on his towel and took off his shoes and entered into the life of the least of these. Having received the free lunch, now it was time to serve it. Charles Stoddard, a writer, dared to visit the colony to see this man who would do such a thing. As Stoddard approached the makeshift chapel, out he came, Father Damien. Stoddard writes, "His priest's cassock was worn and faded, his hair tumbled like a school-boy's; his hands stained and hardened by toil; but the glow of health was in his face, the buoyancy of youth in his manner; while his ringing laugh, his ready sympathy, and his inspiring magnetism told of one who in any sphere might do a noble work."

Who in any sphere might do a noble work. Any sphere? What sphere and what person couldn't use a free lunch? The good, the bad, the ugly? You? Me?

And what to wear to the feast of the king? Faded cassock; damp, dusty towel; shoeless feet—new attire for we who serve the feast.

CHAPTER 3

The Dragon Who Was Sorry

—⁓—

Matthew 18:15–35

HAS THERE EVER BEEN A time in your life when you were not the greatest person to be around? Has there ever been a time when your mood, your anger, your indignation, or your behavior was in such a way that it was just hard for people to be with you, or to like you, or even to reason with you? That how you thought and how you behaved brought about chaos for the people around you? For some of you, I realize that if such a moment ever occurred it was fleeting. Momentary. But I would be willing to bet that there have been times—even for the nicest of us—that there was enough churning deep down inside that as much as we didn't like it, we turned kind of ugly for the people around us. We all have times when we turn sort of ugly and make life difficult. Have you ever made life difficult for someone? It usually happens with the people closest to us or the people we love most, but also complete strangers—people we hope never to see again. I suspect we all can think of times when we made life more difficult for others.

In C. S. Lewis's story *The Voyage of the Dawn Treader*, Lewis tells of a young boy named Eustace who is a rather irascible little lad. Selfish, irritable, never happy, an all-around brat. At one point Eustace is turned into a dragon—a befitting metamorphosis—and for a short while he does not even realize he is a dragon. Then finally he does, and for a few moments he likes the idea of being a dragon. It means he doesn't have to be afraid anymore, and he could be a terror and would be able to get back at all those people he didn't like. But then a few moments later, after this knowledge of being a dragon has sunk in, Eustace all of a sudden doesn't like the idea of being a dragon. Lewis writes about

> the moment [when Eustace thought about getting back at all those people he didn't like] he realized he didn't want to. He wanted to be friends. He wanted to get back among humans and talk and share things. He realized that he was a monster cut off from the whole human race. An appalling loneliness came over him . . . and the poor dragon that had been Eustace lifted up his voice and wept. A powerful dragon crying its eyes out under the moon in a deserted valley is a sight and a sound hardly to be imagined.

There is a little bit of dragon in every one of us, isn't there? Inside each of our lives is a little bit of an ugly monster. Despite whatever outward appearances we may wish to promote, each one of us knows that deep down inside there is a little bit of a monster breathing. Some of us with short fuses have seen the monster leap out almost beyond our control. Some of us are able to keep the monster hidden very well deep down inside—and yet it growls and makes us do things we wished we wouldn't do.

Kathleen Norris, in her book *Amazing Grace*, tells of working with children in a creative writing exercise to get them to articulate their own spirituality. One boy wrote a poem titled, "The Monster Who Was Sorry"—a poem in which the little boy speaks of how angry he gets when he is scolded by his father, and how he has the feelings of a monster and how he wants to wreck his room and wreck his house and even wreck the whole town. Then the poem concludes, "Then I sit in my messy house and say to myself, 'I shouldn't have done all that.'" He is the "monster who is sorry."

Maybe we could all say that about ourselves—that there is a little fire-breathing dragon in every one of us. And we, like the apostle Paul, "do those things which we ought not to do, and don't do those things which we ought to do." We create a mess with our lives, a mess with our dragons' tails. We get ugly and make it hard for even those who love us most to be around us. We look around and see our messy houses and say to ourselves, *I shouldn't have done all this*. Monsters who turn sorry.

It is, I suppose, the reason many of us make our way to church each Sunday. Somewhere along the way we got in touch with the fire-breathing dragon inside our skin. We have been met by the Savior, followed him to the cross, and seen the lengths to which God will go to love us and forgive us. We have heard Jesus' words from the cross: "Father, forgive them for they don't know what they are doing." We have counted ourselves as one of that number—dragons that didn't know what they were doing.

Jesus tells us a story about the slave who has really made a mess of his life—and made a mess of his master's life, too. He has managed to rack up so many debts, put himself in such hock, and put at risk perhaps even his owner's own solvency that the hole he's dug for himself is so deep, there's not a chance of climbing out. His dragon's tail has laid waste all around him. It's a mess he can't clean up. Strangely, he thinks he can. Just give me some more time, he says to the master, and I'll pay it all back. But he can't. Everyone knows he can't. The damage is done. The hole is too deep.

In a stunning development, the master forgives him the damage, erasing the debt and letting him free, with every hope of course that the slave will get the point—that the slave will see how stunning the development really is. "Amazing grace, how sweet the sound that saved a wretch like me." Emphasis on "wretch" and therefore emphasis on "amazing." And this will make all the difference.

But alas, it doesn't. It doesn't make the difference. Because we know the rest of the story—the good turn does not, unfortunately, deserve another. And the slave just can't manage to forgive the peanuts owed by his fellow slave, just can't do it, just can't let this guy slip by. Evidently there is a little more wretch in this guy than there is in me. Somehow he's managed to forget. He's lost the ledger he had with the master, the one with all the red ink; he's managed to lose the big fat IOU torn in two. And with this spiritual amnesia he has developed a laserlike vision for red ink in the other guy. And off to jail you go, pal. Now he's made a mess again.

He's gone off and been a dragon again, and therein lies, doesn't it, the deeper truth about you and me? With this dragon-ness in you and me—this sin, this brokenness, this fire-breathing propensity—though Christ has died for us, though the debt has been wiped clean, though amazing grace has been poured upon us and is beginning to seep into our pores, the truth is that more seeping is left to be done. The stunning development feels less stunning.

Hector Tobar's compelling book *Deep Down Dark* recounts for us the intense story of the disaster that trapped thirty-three Chilean miners underground for ten weeks. We remember the vigil kept for those thirty-three men entombed beneath the earth. And for the first seventeen days, as workers above drilled frantically to find the cavity where the men were imprisoned, the miners struggled to survive with very little food. With each passing day listening to the drilling, lamenting the failed attempts, and growing more desperate, the men found themselves growing into a deep fellowship. They appointed one of their number—the one who appeared most spiritual—to lead them in daily worship, to be their makeshift pastor. They sang, they prayed, and most of all they confessed—all thirty-three of them. They told about their lives to God and to all who would hear the truth. The failings. The selfishness. The poor behavior. The addiction. What they might do if God should rescue them. "We aren't the best men," their pastor prayed over and over again, "but Lord, have pity on us." And when they sang together it was a fellowship and moment of spirit like none had ever experienced. Said one, "When we sang I forgot for a moment that I was trapped in a mine."

But then comes day seventeen, and the drilling strikes the target. A path between heaven and earth is established, and the men know that they have gone, in an instant, from desperate despair to the great chance of being rescued. Two more months they will wait for the drilling to open a large enough shaft for them to be pulled free, but now they can be fed from above. Now there is hope. Tobar chronicles how then the fellowship, once so intimately bound, begins to fall apart. The men begin to fight. Sides are chosen. Worship that once held thirty-three now receives only a half dozen. Some think they were more the hero. Others think they had sacrificed more. Others remember long-held grievances. Quickly forgotten is how equally desperate they had so recently been for mercy. Once mercy had come, mercy had been forgotten.

And that, of course, is the crux: when mercy comes, how quickly it seems to pass.

We've all been there. We are likely there now. We have found on the cross the stunning development—the overwhelming mercy that yearns to seep into our souls—and yet here we are wondering about what the other guy might owe us.

For many of us, the wounds are deep. The debt others have run up on us is enormous. The pain we have endured is extraordinary. The other guy has breathed his fire. But our greatest risk is to somehow lose sight of ourselves in that crowd, the crowd under the cross, that gang of dragons breathing fire at the Savior. It's so easy to lose ourselves in that picture. Monsters making a mess of the world. And to remember that it was to us, it is to us, that the Savior says, "Father, forgive them for they don't know what they are doing."

It may explain why I found it such holy ground when a friend of mine, a recovering alcoholic, invited me to join him at a meeting of his Alcoholics Anonymous group. For years he had been telling me that being in the program had saved his life. I had certainly heard story after story about it from friends and church members who were in the program and what a difference it had made, but I had never stepped inside the communion. I wasn't sure what to expect and was even less sure that I had any place being there. I was not a drinker. But we went. And there we were: rich and poor, young and old, the well-dressed and the rumpled, with the twelve steps before us—the first, of course, being to admit that we were powerless and that our lives had become unmanageable. Second, a Power greater than ourselves could restore us to sanity. As I sat listening to the man before us speaking with brutal honesty about the wreck he had made of his own life and others and his gratitude over his two years of sobriety and his mantra of one day at a time, I felt like I was on holy ground. Never had our humanity felt so real, and never had the power felt so real. None of us had anything over the other. No one better or worse. A sweet communion of the powerless. Dragons who were sorry, yearning for a rescue that comes one day at a time.

Could this be said of us, we who gather before the cross? All debtors. All dragons. All powerless. All in need of a Savior. One day at a time. Father, forgive them for they don't know what they are doing. That this may be said each day *to* us, and that this may be said each day *through* us.

CHAPTER 4

Taking Matters into Your Own Hands

Matthew 4:1–17

THERE IS A CERTAIN GENRE of film and story I remember watching and reading growing up that centers the attention of the narrative on a particular character—the protagonist of the story—whose nature is to be a generally good and law-abiding person. This person believes in right over wrong, justice for the little guy, good over evil. As these stories go, this protagonist spends the first half or two-thirds of the story observing and experiencing and getting angrier and angrier over the evil and injustice around him—until finally he reaches a boiling point and decides to take matters into his own hands. He has had enough, and he is going to single-handedly bring about goodness and justice to the world.

There was the Incredible Hulk—remember him? Mild-mannered Bill Bixby, who always seems to get into some sort of pickle with evil and then all of a sudden muscles start popping and shirts start ripping and eyes start flashing—and boy, you better watch out. Batman, whose movies we are still watching: mild-mannered Bruce Wayne sits back and watches the Joker, the Riddler, Catwoman, and the Penguin mess around with Gotham City until he can take it no more—and then it's down to the Batcave with Robin and the Batmobile, and boy, you better watch out. Clint Eastwood, John Wayne, Bruce Willis, Mel Gibson, Sylvester Stallone—man, you better not heat these guys up to their boiling point or there is no telling what mayhem might ensue.

The constant in all of the stories is this person who has developed such a view of himself—such a sense of self-righteousness, such a perspective of self-perceived clarity—that the only thing he thinks he can do is take matters into his own hands. In fact, the whole story is simply waiting for that moment to happen—when "the man" (though it's not always a man) takes over and saves the day with guns blazing and fists swinging.

As Matthew tells us his good news about Jesus, he spends the first three chapters announcing to us the arrival of the Messiah Jesus—the King of the Jews. Angels announce. Stars align. King Herod panics. And John the Baptist announces and prepares. When the adult Jesus finally arrives on the scene, there is no doubt that Messiah has arrived. He submits to John's baptism. The Spirit alights as a dove. The voice of the Father speaks from the heavens: "This is my beloved Son in whom I am well pleased." Jesus goes even further to prove his mettle by submitting to the movement of the Spirit and being driven into the wilderness where he undergoes forty days of fasting. This is the

Son of God. If anyone has the spiritual and moral authority to take matters into his own hands, Matthew tells us, it's Jesus.

So just when Jesus reaches this height of moral and spiritual character, who should arrive but the devil? The tempter. The adversary. Now is the moment we've been waiting for. Now's the time when the muscles pop and shirts tear. Now's the time when capes are donned and weapons are drawn. Now's the time when the boiling point blows the lid off everything. The great cosmic battle between good and evil, right?

Actually, no. Now is the time for temptation, even though everyone who is reading and everyone who is watching expects the story to go the way the story always goes: God's man takes matters into his own hands, jumps into the wrestling ring, and puts the devil into a headlock. But in God's story this is the time of temptation, the time when we are most vulnerable. Three times the tempter tempts Jesus to take matters into his own hands.

- If you are the Son of God, command these stones to become loaves of bread.
- If you are the Son of God, command the angels to catch you as you fall from the pinnacle of the temple.
- If you are the Son of God, command yourself a following.

If you are the Son of God, take control. Take matters into your own hands. And what Jesus is here to teach us is that when you think you have gotten yourself to some level of moral height, some level of spiritual maturity, some level of unimpeachable character, then you are most susceptible to the tempter and most vulnerable to getting everything wrong. At this point, we begin to rely on ourselves more than on God.

It's how the story of Job begins, right? We all kind of know the story of Job—the man who gets more than his fair share of pain. But the story begins how? It begins by introducing Job as a blameless and upright man who feared God and turned away from evil. Job's the man. He's the one we can count on. He's the blameless one, the righteous one. And he is the one who gets tempted. Death and destruction and disease wipe away everything he holds dear, other than his wife. So now's the time, right? Now's the time to take matters into your own hands. Now's the time to go it alone. Now's the time, says his bride, to curse God and die. Show him that it's not his life anymore; it's yours, and you will flex your muscles and do as you please.

And Job asks—with no muscles bulging, no capes a-furling, no weapons blasting—his simple question, "Shall we receive the good at the hand of God, and not receive the bad?" In other words, we live as God would have us live; we are to be as God would have us be and trust God for the rest. We live as God would have us live and trust God for the rest. We leave the matter in God's hands.

But it is so tempting not to trust God for the rest, right? To take matters into our hands. Take over for the good Lord because doing the right thing doesn't seem to be enough, or to insist that God owes us something. We've done our part, yet somehow we are owed something. More providence. More protection. More reward. More notice. More recognition. Hello, Lord, what about *moi*?

Some of you have heard of J. Hudson Taylor, who was a missionary in China during the nineteenth century. He founded the China Inland Mission, which became the center of Protestant missions in China. After forty-five years in China, Hudson Taylor returned home to England, his native country, and when he landed there in Southampton, he was on the same ship as Teddy Roosevelt. When the ship docked, a band was waiting for Teddy Roosevelt. They played the music and there was confetti and streamers and applause, and Teddy Roosevelt was carried off the ship on the shoulders of his admirers. There was a parade in town for Teddy Roosevelt.

Hudson Taylor just stood there alone, waiting. The church committee that was supposed to meet him never came. Half hour. Hour. Two hours. After two hours he put down his suitcase on the dock and sat down alone.

I didn't expect a band or a cheering mob, he thought, *but there should have been somebody here to welcome me home.*

As Hudson Taylor writes in his diary, "But then God spoke to me. 'Hudson,' he said, 'you're not home yet.'"

It is one of the crazy things about this life—this human life, this human spiritual journey of ours—that as soon as we think we have arrived, as soon as we think we've done what needs to be done, as soon as we think we have some firm grasp of things, that's when the tempter comes. And the only thing that we have to throw at the tempter is not our brains, not our moral superiority, not our wittiness and cunning, not our resume—because those are the very things that the devil in fact uses against us. No, the only thing we can throw at the tempter is humility. An awareness of who we are and whose we are. A deep and abiding sense that we don't have what it takes. Only God has what it takes, and I can only do what God would have me do. And I look to the Son of God in the wilderness—the pioneer and perfecter of our faith, who for the sake of the joy that was set before him endured the tempter; endured the cross, disregarding its shame; and has taken his seat at the right hand of the throne of God. Come down, they said to Jesus up there on that cross. If you are the Son of God, come down! Take matters into your own hands. Make it about you and not about the Father. Show us a little Incredible Hulk.

But from beginning to end Jesus is here as Son of God to teach us about being sons and daughters of God, and sons and daughters of God are very susceptible. We are enormously susceptible to temptation. We are at great risk. The more we think we know God and have been strengthened by some sense of spiritual certitude, we are at greater risk to miss the whole point. Sons and daughters of God by their very nature are happy to leave the certainty to God and the trust to themselves. Certainty to God, trust to themselves. Live as God would have us live and trust God for the rest. As Clint Eastwood's Dirty Harry would say, "A man's got to know his limitations."

Any pastor—we who stand before flocks of folks entrusted to be some sort of authority on the word of God—will tell you how tempting it is to forget one's limitations.

You'll recall the story about the Mississippi riverboat captain who was approached during the Civil War by a cotton trader who asked him if he would run his cotton up the river.

It was illegal to trade cotton then between the North and the South, so the riverboat captain refused. The cotton trader said, "I'll give you five hundred dollars if you run this cotton up the river." The captain said no. "I'll give you a thousand dollars." "No," said the captain. "I'll give you two thousand dollars." No. "I'll give you three thousand dollars." And with that the captain reached for his gun, put it into the man's face, and said, "Get off my boat. You're coming too near my price."

We all have our price, don't we? We all have our limitations. We all have our threshold that may compel us to take matters into our own hands. So, can you hear what the Son of God is saying to the Adversary? Can you hear him speak the word of scripture? Not as weapons. Not as righteous superiority. Not as "I know more than you know." He's quoting so that he can hear. He's uttering the word of God to remember that he is a Son of God. He is not trying to play God; he's trying to obey God. Can you hear it?

- If you are the Son of God, command these stones to become loaves of bread. "It is written, 'One does not live by bread alone, but by every word that comes forth from the mouth of God.'"
- If you are the Son of God, command the angels to catch you as you fall from the pinnacle of the temple. "It is written, 'Do not put the Lord your God to the test.'"
- If you are the Son of God, command yourself a following. "It is written, 'Worship the Lord your God, and serve only him.'"

It's not whether *I* have what it takes, it's whether *God* has what it takes. Only humility can say that.

The greatest leaders of history were women and men who had a sober view of themselves and an exalted view of God.

At one point during the Civil War, Abraham Lincoln issued an authorization to the War Department for a certain transfer of regiments at the front. Secretary of War Edwin Stanton refused to carry out the order from his commander in chief, saying that Lincoln was a fool for issuing the order. When a congressman brought back word that Stanton had called Lincoln a fool, Lincoln replied, "Did Stanton say I was a fool?" "Yes sir," the congressman replied. "He called you a fool several times." Lincoln opined, "Well, if Stanton said I was a fool, then I must be one, because he is nearly always right."

A man's got to know his limitations. We don't play God. We obey God.

It was all that good Baptist preaching, along with wisdom from Mahatma Gandhi, that led Martin Luther King Jr. to employ nonviolence at his tool for change and trust God for the rest. "Nonviolence," he wrote, "is a powerful and just weapon which cuts without wounding and ennobles the man who wields it. It is a sword that heals."

We don't play God. We obey God.

It is, I imagine, what the good apostle Paul had in mind, sitting in Roman house arrest—some friends having let him down, others far away—and the future quite up in the air, with Caesar waving above his head the imperial sword. A good place for the tempter to show up. Curse God and die. Get bitter.

Plan an escape. Give up. Take matters into your own hands. No. No. No. "I have learned," he writes, "to be content with whatever I have. I know what it is to have little, and I know what it is to have plenty. In any and all circumstances I have learned the secret of being well-fed and of going hungry, of having plenty and of being in need. I can do all things through Christ who strengthens me."

It is enough, isn't it? To have Christ with us. To let Christ live in us. To let Christ love through us. To obey God and not to play God.

In those immortal words of Martin Luther,

> Did we in our own strength confide?
>   Our striving would be losing,
> Were not the right man on our side,
>   The man of God's own choosing.
> Dost ask who that may be?
>   Christ Jesus, it is he.

CHAPTER 5

The Real Smallness of Your Greatness

Matthew 3:1–17

Red Klotz died a while ago. He was ninety-three. Red Klotz may not be a name you've ever heard, and he was glad for that to be the case. Klotz was founder, manager, coach, and a player for a basketball team called the Washington Generals. The Washington Generals are the team that he organized to be the perennial opposition to the world-famous Harlem Globetrotters—the comedic basketball phenoms. Every time the Harlem Globetrotters play, and they are still playing, they play the Washington Generals. And every time, the Globetrotters beat the Generals.

The Washington Generals have always been a very good team, filled with former college and NBA players; Red Klotz played on the championship Baltimore Bullets back in the 1940s. But the whole purpose of Red Klotz and the Washington

Generals was to make the Harlem Globetrotters look good. Meadowlark Lemon, Curly Neal, Goose Tatum, and all the rest—even Wilt Chamberlain for a time—would perform their antics on the court and the Generals were the straight guys who helped make the Globetrotters funny. For the Globetrotters to look so good, the Generals had to look a little foolish. Said Klotz, "Laurel had Hardy, Lewis had Martin, Costello had Abbott, and the Trotters have us." The purpose of it all was for the Generals always to come in second to the Globetrotters' first. Except one night back in 1971, Red Klotz by accident made a shot he wasn't supposed to make and the Generals won. Never has a man felt so bad about winning. The Globetrotters didn't mind. Years later the incomparable Meadowlark Lemon said this about Red Klotz: "If anybody calls Red a loser, they're missing the whole point. When a Globetrotter game is over, folks never remember the final score. People remember the laughter."

Red Klotz may have lost every game, but he wasn't a loser. He was part of some bigger victory.

Maybe with his leather girdle, camel's hair clothes, and locust diet, John the Baptist was setting himself up to be called a loser. Out there in the Judean desert—the voice crying in the wilderness—inviting whoever would listen to receive the baptism of repentance—calling the religious leaders snakes. Talk about marginalizing yourself. Talk about the highway to oblivion. Talk about guaranteeing that you'll never get yourself onto a Christmas card. Talk about never getting on the cover of *People* magazine . . . John the Baptist in the eyes of many was walking around with a big L on his forehead.

Isn't it interesting how the good news begins with a loser?

Interesting, isn't it, that of all the Advent figures with the exception of Jesus himself, John the Baptist is the only one who appears in all four Gospels. He doesn't get into any of our Christmas cards or crèches, but he is there in every Advent story. Not that he would have wanted it that way—his whole purpose was to point to someone else—but something about John the Baptist, the pointer, tells us something about the kingdom that Jesus said was at hand. It's how the gospel starts and its how the gospel continues—with those who see themselves as part of some greater story. The gospel starts and the gospel continues when people as unique and as special as they are see themselves as part of God's greater unfolding purpose.

It's that way from the very beginning in Matthew's Gospel. Matthew starts by reminding us of the great, big story. He takes four paragraphs in chapter 1 to tell us of all the generations that preceded Jesus. The fourteen generations from Adam to David. The fourteen generations from David to the exile. The fourteen generations from the exile to Joseph, the father of Jesus. Generations and generations of surprising people who were characters in the great story of God's redemption. And then comes Joseph—who with his pregnant fiancée is happy to bow out of the story, saving his own reputation and pride, but the angel says, "Oh no, Joseph—your life is a part of something greater. Take Mary as your wife." And the good news for Joseph begins when he sees it—when he sees his life as a part of something greater. He submits to the angel's will. The wise men follow the star and make their way to Bethlehem, and Matthew tells us that when they entered the house, they knelt down and worshipped. They saw their lives, their gifts, as part of something greater. Even nasty King Herod—though he didn't want to have any part of the story—finds himself having to submit to the schemes of the angels and can't keep the story from unfolding beneath his very eyes. And then there is John, who with every fabric of his being says when Jesus comes to be baptized, "Oh no . . . this isn't a part of the story. This isn't what the kingdom is about—if there is anyone who will stoop, it will be me." And Jesus says, "That's the point. The kingdom starts for us all when we stoop. The kingdom starts for me when I stoop." For this is what the kingdom of God is: a kingdom of stooping. The new kingdom starts when the new king bows down. This is how the gospel starts and how the gospel continues.

So different from what we might expect, right? Every four years the United States submits herself to a season of presidential candidacy announcements that take place in big places with big crowds with big balloons and big music and big fanfare, and the candidates mount their podiums and tell us how lucky we are that he or she has decided to seek the White House. There is no stooping. No kneeling. No humbling. That's not what that kind of kingdom is about.

But the kingdom of God gets its beginning when John the straight man—John the loser—John the Baptizer—says, "I am not worthy to stoop and untie your sandals." And Jesus says, "You get it. But now's your turn to stand, and for the sake of righteousness, it's my turn to stoop." This is the way the kingdom of heaven begins.

You see, the kingdom of heaven begins in you and in me—not with some sense of false humility or some needless cowering before a power-hungry king. Again, that's Herod's deal. The kingdom of heaven begins when we humbly claim our identity as *children* of God. Not buddies with God. Not co-pilots with God. Not representatives of God. *Children* of God, or dare we say, *toddlers* of God? Not until we see ourselves as children of God, toddlers of God, can we see the wonder and vastness of the Father.

Philips Brooks, the great Boston preacher and composer of "O Little Town of Bethlehem," wrote, "The true way to be humble is not to stoop until you are smaller than yourself, but to stand at your real height against some higher nature that will show you what the real smallness of your greatness is."

The real smallness of your greatness. Only when John can see Jesus for who he is can he see himself for who he really is—and then John can later say about Jesus, "He must increase, and I must decrease."

The first step in the good news for you and me is to get a right view of ourselves. The smallness of our greatness.

I love the story about Ralph Kiner—the great outfielder for the Pittsburgh Pirates decades ago—going to the front office to meet with Branch Rickey, the Pirates owner, to demand a raise. "I hit thirty-seven home runs this year. I led the league in home runs. I want a raise!" Rickey replied, "Ralph, where'd we finish this year?" "Last," said Kiner. "Well," Rickey responded, "we can finish last with you and we can finish last without you."

The smallness of our greatness. The good news starts when we gain a right view of ourselves.

Nelson Mandela spent twenty-seven years as a prisoner of the apartheid regime in South Africa—most of that time in an eight-by-seven-foot cell with a straw mat to sleep on. He was allowed one letter and one visit every six months. In a matter of days of his release, he went on to become first the vaunted leader of the antiapartheid movement—then to becoming a candidate for president, then becoming the first democratically elected leader of the country, and then to being a Nobel Prize winner and world leader. At the top of his world popularity an incident occurred in a visit he made to Shanghai. Staying at a hotel there, Mandela was told that the hospitality staff in that culture would consider it an affront if the former president would not allow them to make his bed. Mandela as a matter of discipline, as a matter of perspective, and as a matter of reminding himself who he was would never allow anyone to make his bed. He made it himself. What to do? Mandela asked if the hotel staff would be gracious enough to give them a moment of their time, especially the maids who were to make his bed. They did. He extended them his appreciation for their service. And would they be kind enough to extend to him one further service? Allow him to make his own bed? They agreed.

The good news begins when you have a right view of yourself. The smallness of your greatness.

Maybe Jesus had it in the back of his mind when he sat at table for the last time with his band of disciples. Realizing that their little world was going to fall apart soon with betrayals and denials and doubts and fleeing, maybe Jesus remembered back to the beginning when John could see the kingdom coming. The kingdom of stooping. The kingdom of seeing that you are a part of something greater. And because none of those men around that table were worthy even to stoop and untie his sandals, Jesus knew what he had to do: stoop and untie theirs. Towel wrapped around him, basin in hand, he washed their feet. A new baptism, shall we call it? Oh no, says Peter, like the loser John—oh no, not me! And Jesus says—oh yes, you. You take part in me only when you let me stoop below you.

The good news begins when you have a clear and right view of yourself. Remember what Meadowlark Lemon said about Red Klotz: "If anybody calls Red a loser, they're missing the whole point. When a Globetrotter game is over, folks never remember the final score. People remember the laughter."

Who had the laugh when, in 1881, not long after he came to be the new president of Tuskegee University, Booker T. Washington was walking through the nicer part of town and a woman on her porch, thinking he was the hired help, called out to the professor, "Would you please come and chop wood for my stove?" Without missing a beat the professor walked over to the woodpile, took off his coat, and started chopping. When a good pile had been assembled, he took it into the house and then went on his way. Later the woman's daughter asked her mother if she knew what she had just done—that she had asked the president of the local college to chop her some wood. The woman was mortified and the next morning appeared in Washington's office. Apologizing profusely, she said repeatedly,

"I did not know it was you I put to work." Washington replied, "It's entirely all right, madam. I like to work, and I am delighted to do favors for my friends and neighbors."

Who had the laugh? It's not the final score that matters, it's the laughter they remember. The smallness of our greatness.

CHAPTER 6

The Climb

—~~—

Matthew 5:1–20

ON DECEMBER 27, 2014, A couple of rock climbers, Tommy Caldwell and Kevin Jorgenson, set out to be the first two people to free climb the straight vertical ascent of the Dawn Wall of the El Capitan mountain in Yosemite National Park. No one had ever been able with bare hands and no benefit of pull ropes to make it to the top. Ever. The ascent took nineteen days. Nineteen days sleeping on the sheer cliff of this mountain, hanging tents on the side of the mountain and sleeping suspended in midair. It meant many failed pitches from one point of the cliff face to another, which meant many failed attempts, which meant many slams of their bodies against the stone wall: bruises and abrasions and cuts and discouragement. But after seven years of preparing and nineteen days climbing, they stepped foot on the summit and accomplished what many describe as the greatest ascent ever in human history. To view this rock face it seems incomprehensible that any human being could ever come close—not to mention make it to the top. But they did. And they did because they tried. They took the first step.

Sometimes the first step is the hardest.

I am guessing that we all have in each of our lives a few El Capitans. Over the course of our days we have looked ahead to some difficult or impossible journey—some insurmountable summit, some massive endeavor—and have wondered to ourselves not only whether it was possible but whether it was even worth trying. Maybe it was some sort of physical challenge—running a marathon, climbing Kilimanjaro, swimming a mile, through-hiking the Appalachian Trail. Such feats are probably the dream of only a few of us. But for the rest of us, the difficult journeys often have to do with what is going on inside. Journeys of the mind and journeys of the heart.

I ran into a seventy-year-old man a while back who wondered to himself whether he could learn to speak French. He wasn't particularly good at languages, but maybe he could teach himself. Quite a climb. Some wonder about starting a business. Some dream about writing a book. Some imagine trying to make some difference in the world—feeding the hungry, putting a dent in human trafficking, teaching the disadvantaged, changing the spiral of poverty in Honduras. Quite a climb. Some look into their personal world and see some El Capitans—relationships that need scaling, hurts that need healing, sins that need forgiving. And the climb seems pretty steep, nearly impossible, and standing at the base makes you wonder if it's even worth taking the first step.

Whatever it might be, each of us harbors some yearning to scale some sort of height.

Now, when it comes to the El Capitans of our lives, the resistance about taking the first step often has to do just as much with us as it does with the scale of the climb. I am guessing that a part of all of us has been convinced along the way of all the things we cannot do. The further you get along in life, the more loudly the voice gets in your head that insists that you are just not capable of taking on the climb. Too steep. Too difficult. Too comprehensive. Too expensive. Too complicated. Too dangerous. Too much for this little brain—whatever it might be. And because we can't imagine tackling all of it, we never even start.

Recall Eleanor Roosevelt's line: "No one can make you feel inferior without your consent."

Charles Schulz, the creator of the comic strip *Peanuts*, when reflecting on the genesis of Charlie Brown often referred back to his childhood and his sense that his parents didn't believe in him. He figured that they didn't believe in him because they didn't believe in themselves. Thinking about his mother, Schulz once said, "She didn't go to PTA meetings because she did not feel she was sophisticated enough to mingle with the other parents. . . . Maybe because she went no further than the third grade. . . . She felt that she did not have the right type of clothes. . . . It would have been wonderful if someone could have explained to my mother that she need not have felt inadequate." No surprise that *Peanuts* carried for fifty years the theme of Charlie Brown and his inadequacy. And no surprise that it became the most-read comic strip in American history. We all have some sense of inadequacy.

And maybe more than anywhere else in our lives, our sense of inadequacy reaches its highest level when it comes to our relationship with God and the journey of the spirit. The life of being a disciple. Pews in every church are filled with people who look at the spiritual journey and wonder if the climb is too steep, the trail too long, the ascent too dangerous. And in thinking of all those things that God might desire of us, we consider the mountain and say it's not worth the first step.

Nowhere might we feel this inadequacy greater than in the three chapters we find in Matthew that tradition calls the Sermon on the Mount. The Sermon on the Mount, relayed only in Matthew, is a 110-verse collection of Jesus' teaching. To read it is to hear from Jesus of the El Capitan of the discipleship life. In verse after verse Jesus presents to us the height and depth and breadth of the spiritual journey, the pinnacle of the spiritual climb—the high bar of following Jesus, so high that once you read through the Sermon on the Mount one of your first feelings is that the mountain is too high. Pick just a few verses: Jesus says, "If you say, 'You fool,' to your brother or sister, you will be liable to the hell of fire." "If you look at a woman with lust you have committed adultery with her in your heart." "If someone strikes you on the right cheek, turn the other also." "Love your enemy." "Do not judge." "Do not store up treasures on earth." "Don't be worried about tomorrow." Makes El Capitan look like a walk in the park! And what we might want to say to ourselves is, *Why start? What's the point? I can't be all those things. I can't become this person Jesus wants me to be.* "Be perfect as your Father in heaven is perfect," Jesus says. Not going to happen, so why even try?

And maybe that's the reason why when Jesus begins his Sermon on the Mount—this El Capitan of the spiritual life—he begins with these introductory statements about the blessed life we call the Beatitudes: twelve verses in which we learn about the blessed life. And what we discover is that the blessed life has very little to do with whether you get to the top—and everything to do with whether you have started. The blessed life is about the journey to become children of God. Blessed are you if you start the climb, because when you start climbing you start becoming. And if you start becoming—here's what might happen:

- You might find that you lack in spirit—but blessed are you for the climb is full of spirit and grace.
- You might find yourself grieving and mourning—but blessed are you because the climb gets your heart breaking for the world.
- You might hunger and thirst for righteousness—but blessed are you, for the climb gets you hungering and thirsting for the right things.
- You might have to be merciful—but blessed are you, because the climb of mercy will show you how much you need for yourself.

- You might have to bring peace to a frayed and tearing world—but blessed are you, because the climb of peacemaking brings to you a little peace for yourself.

But, you see, all of it comes in the climb. All of it comes when we stop standing and staring at the cliff and start the ascent.

"Costly grace" is what Bonhoeffer called it. If we would ever hope for this blessed life that God would promise us, it comes not just in the accepting of the grace of Christ—saying yes to Jesus' forgiveness—but in saying yes to the climb. The setting out. Jesus invites us into the ascent—with all its slips and falls and pitches and hanging in midair, and bumps and bruises and scratches—but all that comes with the blessed life. It's not about the top; it's about the incredible climb!

Tommy Caldwell, one of those El Capitan climbers, put it this way: "I came to the point a few years ago where I figured it was worth it whether we made it or not. I just loved the way that it made me live, so I decided to push forward as long as it kept making me feel that way. Actually doing it was really the icing on the cake."

It was worth it whether we made it or not. I just loved the way it made me live.

A wonderful couple I know—whom I married almost twenty years ago—decided a few years back that they weren't getting any younger (they're around forty) and that at the top of their bucket list was bicycling together completely around the globe. They decided to do it, and for several years they had to go through the arduous process of preparation: saving money, selling their house, buying equipment, mapping the course, and so on. Then came the day when they put foot to pedal . . . and they started. They set out. They started from the state of Washington, crossing North America, taking a ship across the ocean, and had gone as far as Africa in nine months. *Africa!* And with those nine months and those miles came incredible stories of peril and adventure and life-transforming experiences. A couple of weeks later a family issue arose that meant they had to store their bikes, pack up their stuff, and come home. They don't know for how long and they don't know if they will be able to resume. But, as they said, it doesn't matter! They got to Africa, for God's sake. And the way to get to Africa is to take the first pedal.

Thomas Merton, the great twentieth-century ascetic, gave up the urbane life to become a Trappist monk. In his autobiography *The Seven Storey Mountain*, while reflecting upon his decision to take those first steps, Merton shares this prayer he made to God: "I was not sure," Merton prays, "where I was going, and I could not see what I would do when I got [there]. But you saw further and clearer than I, and you opened the seas before my ship, whose track led me across the waters to a place I had never dreamed of, and which you were even then preparing to be my rescue and my shelter and my home. . . . How far have I to go to find You in Whom I have already arrived!"

How far I have to go to find You in Whom I have already arrived.

And it all begins with setting out. So what about it? What will it look like for you to take the next step into the blessed life? To make your advance upon the great and holy mountain before you? To read those 110 verses of Jesus' great sermon and pick just one thing and say, "This is what I will do." What might that mean for this great church if together we took our own next steps? At the beginning of another year, what light and salt we would be in the world if you and I started climbing. I mean really climbing. Ascending. Living into the costly grace. Putting hands to the stone and pulling upward. Living into the blessed life—feeling the dangerous thrill of taking the chance. Rearranging your sedentary schedule. Redoing your comfortable budget. Expanding your sleepy mind. Putting to work your slow beating heart. Hungering, thirsting, peacemaking, mourning, giving mercy. Oh my Lord, there's no telling what might happen if we put foot to pedal—if we looked upward and stepped the first step. Scary, yes! Risky, yes! Uncertain, yes! Blessed? Yes, says Jesus. But will we?

Stephen Ambrose, in his great book on Meriwether Lewis and the Lewis and Clark expedition, quotes from Lewis's journal as he started into what he knew was going to be the most dangerous and uncertain journey of his life. Lewis wrote, "We are now about to penetrate a country at least two thousand miles in width, on which the foot of civilized man has never yet trod; the good or evil it has in store for us is, for experiment, as yet to be determined .... I can but esteem this moment of my departure as among the most happy of my life."

Blessed are those who take the first step.

CHAPTER 7

The Tell-Tale Heart

Matthew 6:7–21

If you are a tennis fan, you may have caught the little story that took place a while back during the Australian Open. US tennis player Tim Smyczek was playing for his life—his tennis life, anyway. The young man from Milwaukee was ranked 112th in the world and was up against perhaps the world's greatest tennis player at the time, Rafael Nadal. Young Smyczek played the match of his life, taking the tennis giant to five sets and was one game away from winning. With everything on the line and Nadal serving in the final game, a spectator shouted in the middle of Nadal's serve, disrupting his rhythm and causing the serve to land out—an unfortunate turn for the champion that could very well have sent the match against him. But Smyczek, the underdog—under no obligation from the rules and at great risk of giving away the moment of his life—held up two fingers to the judge, the signal to give the champion the serve back. Request granted. Nadal served, won the point, and two points later won the match and sent the young American home—nary a footnote in tennis history.

In the wake of all the silly stories we read and hear about in sports—steroids, deflated footballs, gazillion-dollar contracts—it's good to be reminded that there are still some quiet and heroic gestures of fairness in the world.

Smyczek's story reminds me of the two-man Italian bobsled team in the Innsbruck 1964 Olympics. They had just finished their second run in record time, putting themselves for the moment in first place before the last run. Up on top of the hill, the British team was preparing for its final run when it was discovered that the axle bolt to their sled has snapped off, rendering it impossible to go down the mountain. When news came to the bottom of the mountain to Eugenio Monti, the Italian captain, that the Brits had this terribly unfortunate circumstance, Monti went to his sled, detached his axle bolt, and sent it up to the Brits to fix their sled. The Brits had an incredible final run and won the gold medal.

Stories like these are obvious examples of great sportsmanship, but they are also stories that tell the tale of the heart. There is nothing like a public moment when so much of who you are and so much of what you want for yourself are set up against so much of who you are and so much of what you want for yourself. Who wouldn't want the gold medal, and who wouldn't want to be the greatest in the land? Why, we would give anything—including maybe our souls. Times such as these—when just a turn of the head or a shrug of the shoulders would get you the trophy—require a person to locate the heart. Who am I really? What do I really want out of this life? What am I really called to do? Stories that tell the tale of the heart.

Years ago I had the chance to walk the floor of the New York Stock Exchange with a friend who was a trader on the floor. We've all seen pictures of the floor of the New York Stock Exchange—a pretty chaotic place with hundreds of people placing trades. At one point as we were moving from one part of the floor to the next, my friend was pulled aside by another trader. For the next ninety seconds outside of my hearing there ensued a rather intense exchange between the two. When my friend returned he was silent for several minutes as we continued to walk, and then he proceeded to tell me what had just happened—that his fellow trader was trying to convince him to do something just a little bit illegal. Not much and likely never to be discovered, but wrong nevertheless. He had declined. He said, "I get those kinds of offers about once a week. And every week it gives me the chance to check again my soul."

It is the soul that Jesus turns to again and again in his Sermon on the Mount. Verse after verse, it seems, point to all these moments in your life and mine that tell the tale of our hearts. Our souls. The Sermon on the Mount is this great cardiac exam. Let's talk, Jesus says, about your heart.

- If you're letting yourself get angry to the point of calling someone a fool—well, then that is a tale of the heart.
- If you find your attention drawn to someone outside of your marriage, that is a tale of the heart.

- If you find yourself harboring a grudge against an enemy, that is a tale of the heart.
- If you are more interested in people seeing how good you are, that is a tale of the heart.
- If you are having trouble forgiving someone, that is a tale of the heart.
- If you are trying to serve two masters, that is a tale of the heart.

Likewise, Jesus says, when it comes to the challenge and blessing of treasure—financial treasure—no surprise . . . it is a story that tells the tale of the heart. "Do not store up for yourselves treasures on earth where moth and rust consume. But store up treasures in heaven where neither moth nor rust consume."

Where your treasure is, there will your heart be also.

The big mistake you and I make when it comes to this teaching of Jesus about treasure and heart is that we go only as far with this teaching as makes us feel guilty. There are treasures on earth and treasures in heaven, and it seems like I have more treasures on earth than I do in heaven—so I'm a bad person and I hope God forgives me. That's as far as we let that teaching take us. But that's not the point. Jesus doesn't come to make us guilty. Jesus comes to wonder with us where we want our hearts to be. Jesus comes to help us check our souls. Where is your heart taking you, and is that where you want it to be? When push comes to shove, where do you want your heart beating most?

A friend of mine tells the story of his lusting after the latest version of a BMW motorcycle. I don't know enough about motorcycles to describe one of these bikes, but he tells of making the decision to buy the model he'd been ogling for years. And he tells of feeling his heart pounding with joy as he signed the papers, started the engine, and drove off the lot. He drives it into the garage, goes into the house, and on the kitchen table is the mail. In the mail is the brand-new BMW catalogue for the next year's model. As my friend describes it, he felt his heart slow to almost a stop. Long before rust and moth consumed, he had already lost his heart.

So Jesus wonders with us about where we want our hearts beating most. In other words, with whom do we wish to have our love affair? In particular, Jesus wonders about the love affair we might have with our Father in heaven. It's not that we shouldn't enjoy the things of the earth in some sort of moderation, but what might it mean that with each passing day and week and year our hearts would grow larger for God? What would happen if this heart inside of us grew larger and larger for the things God seems most concerned about—that we could grow to become unashamed fans of God? "Our Father, who art in heaven, hallowed be thy name. Thy kingdom come, thy will be done, on earth as it is in heaven." That's the start of fandom. What if we became these outrageous fans for the kingdom of God? That despite whatever pressures we might feel to be something or someone else—give away our souls—we would have this strong and beating heart for the Father? That whatever we might do in public or private, we would wish to please the Father? God doesn't want to guilt us into giving. He wants to grow us into giving.

I am a University of Michigan football fan, so let's imagine something that for some seems unimaginable: the Michigan football team is playing for the national championship. (I think Jesus will come back before this happens, but suspend disbelief and imagine it happening.) The game is sold out, and I get a call from a friend who has a ticket for me—and it only costs a thousand dollars. Now, any motivation I might have to pay that thousand dollars will come not because of guilt. You can't guilt me to pay that money for a dumb football game. No, the only motivation comes from my fandom. It comes from my heart. The heart gets us to do some crazy things. The heart gives back the serve to the champion. The heart sends an axle bolt up the mountain. The heart says no to a shady deal. The heart gets us to do some crazy things, and the crazy things have everything to do with who you are rooting for.

It makes me think of the high school football game my brother was playing in. I was up in the stands watching with my mother, and my father was down on the sidelines watching the game from up close. And then it happened. My brother intercepted the football and had in front of him a clear fifty-yard path to the end zone. So off he sprinted—and the only thing I can remember about that moment was not watching my brother running to the end zone, but watching my father—in the suit and tie of the supposedly respected pastor, raincoat flapping in the air, cheering at the top of his voice—my father with no thought to anything else but his boy, running down the sidelines with him.

Where your treasure is, there will your heart be also.

"See what love the Father has for us that we should be called children of God." God is our biggest fan. And he gives us the honor to cheer him back. To love him with all our hearts, all our minds, all our strength, and all our souls. For this, Jesus says, is what life is all about. These hearts pounding for God.

For where your treasure is, there will your heart be also.

CHAPTER 8

It's the Gift That Counts

—~~—

Isaiah 42:1–9

Not many know the name or the person behind the name of Scott Fahlman. Scott Fahlman, it is widely believed, is the creator of the first smiley emoticon and the first frowny emoticon. An emoticon is an emotional icon, a symbol that expresses emotion. If I were to draw a smiley face or a frowny face, that would be an emoticon—a symbol or image that expresses one's emotion. In this hypertypographical world, we are relying more and more upon emoticons—typing symbols—often using punctuation marks—that express the emotion behind our words. In some text or email that we send—especially when there is the chance that our words could be misread as expressing an unintended emotion—we add an emoticon to try to convey the feeling behind the words. Emoticons have been around for a long time—long before we even ended our letters and notes with "XXOO." We can trace them back to the days of Morse code. But Scott Fahlman is the Carnegie Mellon computer scientist who came up with the idea of using a colon, a dash, and a right parenthesis to represent a smiley-face emoticon, and a colon, dash, and left parentheses to represent a frowny-face emoticon. And he came up with this in 1982, over thirty years ago!

Fast-forward a few years to Bill Gates, Steve Jobs, and Mark Zuckerberg, the creators, respectively, of Microsoft, Apple, and Facebook—not to mention a host of others who have created all sorts of electronic media that we depend upon more and more to communicate with one another—and we find ourselves in this world of hypertypography. We are people of the text—the text we compose in an email, the content we compose in a text message, the text we read on a blog, the text we read on our Kindles. We are people of the word, and in being so, we are not unlike the people of God from long ago who were people of the word, people of the text. The sacred texts. The Torah. The Prophets. The Law and the Prophets, Jesus called them. Israel was a nation of the text—the sacred text, a text long ago that was in the hands of only a very few: the scholars whose job it was to study the text and eke out of it every last drop of meaning and to discern the spirit inside the text. All this—imagine—without emoticons! No smiley faces or frowny faces in the Bible. Just the text.

And so the sacred text found in Isaiah 42 imagines in the unfolding of God's great story a servant—a chosen one—one whose very being will host the spirit of God and bring justice.

This quiet servant's mission is to bear gently and model faithfully the will of God for all the nations to see. For hundreds of years when Israel read and studied that text, they believed that this servant was Israel herself, the people of Israel, and that as a nation they were the servant of God to the world. But then in his Gospel—as he tells the story of Jesus—Matthew looks into the text and sees something else. He connects the dots between the servant in Isaiah and the rabbi Jesus. It is Jesus who is the chosen one, whose very being hosts the spirit of God, who enfleshes the person of God, and who will enact God's justice. In Jesus we see the servant who bears gently and models faithfully the will of God—for all the world to see.

And when you begin to get your heart and mind around the notion that Jesus is the enfleshment of God, we see something world-changing happening—because now God has chosen to speak not just in text but in flesh. Skipping the whole step of emoticon—smiley, frowny, XXOO—God chooses not some punctuation marks in the sky but rather God inhabits the text and the world with flesh and blood. The reason we might call this world-changing is that God is saying something about himself that he cannot say in text. He can't spell this out. God is saying that his own fullest expression cannot be done unless in person. Personality cannot be expressed fully except in person. God so loved the world that he didn't send a text. God so loved the world that he didn't just say, "Read the book." God so loved the world that the personality of God showed up in person. God so loved the world that he went far beyond the smiley face in the sky.

You see, it just has to be the case that the deep-down reason why you and I get so drawn into the gravitational pull of Christmas and the story of Jesus' birth is that there is something so right, so true, and so rational about what happens in Bethlehem. If God is truly God, he must show up in person. God so loved the world that he showed up. Personality shows up in person.

We know it deep down to be true. If you want to show who you really are—if you want to really express what is inside—text and emoticons are one thing, but when we show up, arrive in the flesh, and let flesh touch flesh, then true personality is revealed.

Doesn't it say something about me and you when we arrive in the flesh? I was visiting the hospital awhile ago. I walked into the little eatery, and sitting there was someone I knew, sipping on some coffee and reading a book. I asked her what she was doing. She told me that her dear friend was upstairs keeping vigil over her dying mother. "I thought to myself," she said, "it wasn't enough for me to text. I felt I needed to be here for her. Every hour or so I go up and take her something just for her to know that somewhere in this building, someone is here for her."

When we join the shepherds and make our way into the Bethlehem Nativity and see the vulnerable little baby, what we see is God wanting to be in relationship with us—real, live, and in the flesh—because that's where God engages us in our deepest places . . . and draws from us our deepest selves.

Flesh will do that to you. Think of the people closest to you, your deepest relationships, and think of how deeply they engage you and draw from you. Think of the potential of how deeply they can make you happy, make you sad, give you joy, make you disappointed, stir you, and even change you. No other gift does this like the flesh.

I was walking through the mall the other day, and two guys were standing there and watching the latest flat-screen, digital, high-definition, ten-thousand-inch television set. The expression on their faces said, "Now that's what I want for Christmas." Now I get it. The TV I have in my house is bigger than I could have ever imagined thirty years ago. And it sure is nice to see every freckle on every face and to say, "Boy, looks like real life." But of course it isn't. There is no flesh. There is no soul. There is no touch. There is no breath. There is no stir *inside* our souls.

Remember that wonderful scene in the movie *A Beautiful Mind*—the story of Nobel Prize–winner John Nash's struggle with paranoid schizophrenia—in which he keeps hearing voices and seeing people appear who don't really exist? When is finally at the end of his rope, not truly knowing what is delusion and what is real, his wife comes to him and says, "Do you want to know what's real?" And she takes his hand and puts it to her face and her heart and says, "This is real."

So God steps onto the scene, taking our hand and placing it to his face, to his heart, and says, "This is real." When we see Jesus weeping at the tomb of his dear friend Lazarus, we imagine him sitting at our kitchen table weeping with us in our loss of a loved one. When we see Jesus red-faced and upturning tables in his effort to cleanse the temple, we imagine him red-faced and in *our* face, angry over our choice to monetize the meaning of life. When we see Jesus sweating drops of blood in the Garden of Gethsemane, we imagine him sweating with us as we struggle with what we think to be a life-and-death decision. When we see Jesus place his hands upon the eyes of the blind man, we imagine him pressing his flesh to ours, to our hurts and wounds, and speaking the healing word. When we see Jesus breaking bread and pouring the cup, when we see Jesus breaking his body and pouring his blood, we imagine "what wondrous love is this that caused the Lord of bliss to bear the dreadful curse for my soul."

Do you see, really, how much God loves us? Do you see the good news of what is behind what we call the incarnation? Do you see the outlandish event that Christians believe—that God became flesh and like an unsettled baby demands our attention? God became flesh and rings the front doorbell of our houses. We can hide behind our screens and our phones and our keyboards and our texts, but there is one who puts his hand upon us and says, "This is real."

Undoubtedly you've seen news clips of children whose military mothers and fathers—months away in the theaters of war—return to surprise their children with a visit or a final homecoming. One in particular is emblazoned in my mind. It happens in a classroom. A boy is sitting at his desk facing the board up at the front, but he doesn't know that his father, a year away at war, is standing at the back. Enough ruckus is made to cause the boy to turn, and there is his father. In the flesh. And the expression. Oh my lord, the expression. And then the sprint and the face buried in Daddy's belly. And the sobs. No text, Skype, or emoticon can make that happen. Only the flesh.

The people of Scripture—you and me—know that God is mighty, loving, and powerful. We hear, "The virgin will conceive and bear a son . . . and she will call him Immanuel, which means, 'God is walking in the back of the classroom.'" For this is the gift that counts: that the God who breathed life into us is with us still to breathe life upon us each and every day. When we laugh, he laughs. When we cry, he cries. When we don't know what to do, when life gets too hard, he gently sits with us. When we hurt, he heals. When we sin, he forgives.

For in the beginning was the Word . . .
    And the Word became flesh . . .
        And the Word has slipped into the classroom . . .
            Full of grace and truth.

CHAPTER 9

The Principle of Peter, Paul, and Mary

—∿∿—

Acts 14:8–18

LAURENCE JOHNSTON PETER WAS A professor of education at the University of Southern California fifty years ago. While doing research, he noticed a pattern that exists in generally all organizations and corporations—the best and the worst: a pattern of personnel promotion that seemed nearly always to result in the same outcome. Peter observed that people in just about any organization or corporation were being promoted all the way up to the level where they were ultimately incompetent. Promotions took place not for what people could do but for what they had done. If you were a good clerk, they promoted you to manager. If you were a good manager, they promoted you to executive. If you were a good executive, they promoted you to president. You were promoted all the way to the point where the job was bigger than your talent. Then, in most cases, you'd be fired for attempting to do what the organization thought you could do even though you couldn't. Laurence Johnston Peter wrote a book called *The Peter Principle*, in which he clearly explained, "Every employee tends to rise to his level of incompetence. . . . In time every post tends to be occupied by an employee who is incompetent to carry out its duties. . . . [The real] work is accomplished by those employees who have not yet reached their level of incompetence."

This principle is humbling when you are the senior pastor of a church. Hmmm. Every employee tends to rise to his level of incompetence? I can only imagine what my colleagues are thinking.

Such a reality is humbling for all of us, is it not? Countless are the conversations that you and I have been in when someone has said (and often that someone is us), "Man, I could do a better job than that. Just give a few days, and I'd fix things!" You have no idea, for example, what a blessing I would be to a major league baseball team if I was just given the chance to manage. I'd be such a blessing to our country if I was just given the chance to be president. What a blessing I would be given the chance to bring peace to the Middle East.

But you and I are limited. Each of us has a level of incompetence, and if you don't think you're limited, then step off a cliff and see how well you fly. Find the cure for cancer. Create life. Manage the Chicago Cubs to a World Series championship. Some things just can't be done. It's the Peter Principle.

The apostles Paul and Barnabas—without benefit of Laurence Peter's principle—were faced with, shall we say, a crisis of personnel promotion. These two followers of Jesus made their way to the town of Lystra and found there a man crippled from birth. Having heard the disciples' testimony that Jesus had healed the sick, Paul and Barnabas understood that they were to somehow come alongside this crippled man and bring to him a healing word. They believed that the spirit of Jesus was available to all, and knowing that the spirit of Jesus was a healing spirit, they sensed their call. Seeing in the man's eyes an eagerness to be made well, they offered to him a healing and hopeful word: Get up and walk. And the result of the healing word was indeed healing. Imagine that. The healing word was healing, and the crippled man rose and walked. Something had happened.

Now activate the Peter Principle. Time for a promotion. The Lycaonians see in Paul and Barnabas room for advancement. Let's make them gods! Zeus has come down. Hermes is upon us. We are in the presence of the gods! And who could blame those Lycaonians. It's not often you see crippled men walking. Some power these guys got. They look like humans, talk like humans, and smell like humans, but let's make them more than what they are! Let's promote them beyond their ability.

That's an amazing place to be. Not everybody can get a crowd thinking that they're gods. And so we hear hints of Jesus in the wilderness. Very God of Very God. He's in the wilderness with no fear of any Peter Principle, and here comes the tempter, who dangles before Jesus the great temptation we all face—that we might think of ourselves more highly than we should. That we might take the bait and make ourselves into gods. So tempting: To listen to your own reviews, to read your own press releases, to say, "Well, maybe they're right. Maybe I could run this show better. No Achilles' heel here! I got this under control. Maybe I really am what they think I am!"

I read sometime back about the online marketing world and that more and more companies are getting people to post good reviews on their website. It's what we do, right? We go online to check out a hotel or a restaurant or a book to see if it has good reviews. So now there is a cottage industry of "reviewers" who are happy to write you a good review at a price! Fifty bucks gets you a good review. Fifty bucks gives you and everybody else a false sense of who you are. But perception is more important than reality.

Paging through the New Testament you'll find person after person, character after character, confronting the very possibility that maybe they are not what people think they are. In the story of the good news for Gentiles, Cornelius bows down and worships Peter, and Peter says, "Whoa, whoa, wait a second. You got the wrong guy. I'm just as mortal as the rest of them." The Lycaonians worship who they think are Zeus and Hermes, and Paul and Barnabas say, "Whoa, whoa, you got the wrong guys. We're just as mortal as the rest of them." Page after page it is the principle of Peter and Paul and Mary and Barnabas and James and John—people who have had to confront who they really are and realize that if the good news is to occur, it's going to come through some damaged goods.

Do you imagine about yourself that you are damaged goods? A clay jar, as Paul would call it—the one who called himself the least of the apostles? We have this treasure in clay jars. We are susceptible to cracking up. We have our stressor points. We may have that glaze on the surface, but we can shatter at the slightest nudge. But therein lies the good news, right? The punch line delivered over and over again in the pages of God's great story is that it is never what we end up making of ourselves; it's what God ends up making of us.

Can you picture that early church in the wake of the resurrection, those disciples and apostles looking around at their motley crew and saying to themselves, *He wants us to make disciples of all nations? Us? We who have just run from him, doubted him, denied him, betrayed him—and now he thinks that this crew will announce the good news?* Talk about the Peter Principle, the Paul Principle, the Mary Principle. And maybe that's why Mary had to be the one who stumbled upon the empty tomb. Poor, unqualified Mary. Demon-possessed Mary. Second-class-woman Mary. She didn't ask to be the Christian church's first preacher. It just happened—God using the least likely, the least expected, to bring about the power and the glory. We have this treasure in these clay jars. And maybe that's the point, Paul says, so that it can be shown that the extraordinary power belongs not to us but to God. Zeus? No. Hermes? No. Broken clay jar? Well, of course.

I love the story that Bill Harley relates about the least of the apostles. He tells about attending his son's T-ball games and watching the struggle of all different kinds of children learning to play the national pastime. A girl he calls Tracy wasn't very good and wore Coke-bottle glasses and had a hearing aid in one ear. She ran clumsily and fielded nonexistently. But everybody cheered for her just for the fact that she was trying. And every time she got up to bat she would swing and miss, or hit the tee and the ball would drop to the ground. But Tracy didn't much care. She was just glad to be there.

But then the day came when Tracy actually hit the ball—*really* hit the ball. And because it was Tracy at the bat, all the fielders had been playing in. By some incredible grace the ball not only squirted through the infield but made its way past the outfielders. The crowd went crazy. Everybody on both sides began screaming and cheering for Tracy. "Run, Tracy, run!" So she loped down to first base with the coach swinging his arm wildly for her to keep going; so she turned toward second and kept running. The fielders from the other team were scurrying to catch up to the ball as Tracy made her way to second. She stopped at second, and the third-base coach screamed for her to keep going. So she started for third, and by this time in true T-ball fashion the ball was being thrown wildly and dropped plentifully and Tracy was on her way to third. And then, to quote Harley, "Adults fell out of the bleachers." *Go, Tracy, go!* Tracy reached third and stopped. Her coach stood at home plate calling her as the ball passed over the first baseman's head and landed in the fielding team's empty dugout. "Come on, Tracy! Come on, baby! Get a home run!"

Tracy started for home, and then it happened. During the pandemonium, no one had noticed the geriatric mutt that had lazily settled itself down in front of the bleachers five feet from the third-base line. As Tracy rounded third, the dog, awakened by the screaming, sat up and wagged its tail at Tracy as she headed for home. The tongue hung out, mouth pulled back in an unmistakable canine smile, and Tracy stopped right there. Halfway home, thirty feet from a legitimate home run.

She looked at the dog. Her coach called, "Come on, Tracy! Come on home!" He went to his knees behind the plate, pleading. The crowd cheered, "Go, Tracy, go! Go, Tracy, go!" She looked at all the adults, at her own parents shrieking and catching it all on video. She looked at the dog. The dog wagged its tail. She looked at her coach. She looked at home. She looked at the dog. Everything went to slow motion. She went for the dog! It was a moment of complete, stunned silence. And then—perhaps not as loud, but deeper, longer, and more heartfelt—they all applauded as Tracy fell to her knees to hug the dog.

Despite their cheers to the contrary, everybody knew that Tracy made the right choice.

We have this treasure in clay jars: the least likely can be the bearers of the surprising good news.

Did you know that you don't have to be anyone other than yourself? You don't have to be raised to your level of incompetence. You don't have to prove what you are not. You don't have to pay for a good review. It isn't you; it is Christ in you.

The rabbis would say, "Better a sinner who knows he's a sinner than a saint who knows he's a saint."

Martin Buber recounted the old Hasidic tale about the rabbi named Zusya who died and went to stand before the judgment seat of God. As he waited for God to appear, he grew nervous thinking about his life and how little he had done. He began to imagine what God was going to ask him: "Zusya, why weren't you Moses or why weren't you Solomon or why weren't you David?" But when God finally appeared the rabbi was surprised to hear God say, "Zusya, why weren't you Zusya?"

We hold this treasure in clay jars, so that it may be made clear that this extraordinary power belongs to God and does not come from us.

CHAPTER 10

Emptying Out the Theater

Matthew 6:1–34

When I was a young boy my church had a Christmas pageant. We had one every year—one of those old-time Christmas pageants that enacted the Nativity story. I participated in this pageant in nonspeaking parts for years: a sheep one year, a goat another year, a camel, a silent wise man. I waited patiently as I ascended through elementary school until the sixth grade, when I would be given the chance for a speaking part. There were two male speaking parts. The first was the lead shepherd who got to say, "Let us go unto Bethlehem to see this thing which the Lord has made known to us." The second was the angel Gabriel who got to come out at the beginning of the entire production with big floppy wings strung to his back and a halo pinned to his hair and he had this rather lengthy monologue wherein he announced to Mary that she was going to have a child. It was the biggest part of the play and I wanted it. I wanted the lines, the wings, the halo. And because my father was pastor of the church I knew the part was mine. I was unaware of the word "nepotism," but I assumed its benefits in my heart and soul. Long before the role assignments I had already committed half the part to memory.

Imagine my surprise when the part of Gabriel went to my best buddy, Danny McIlroy. I was dumbfounded. Had I not made it clear to my father that I wanted that part? Did he not understand his paternal obligation? Later I came to learn that it was precisely to avoid any charges of nepotism that the Gabriel part was steered past me and to my friend. I was left with the shepherd's speech, "Let us go unto Bethlehem and see this thing which the Lord has made known to us." And it was with about that much enthusiasm that on that Advent Sunday afternoon I began to recite my line, my one brief line—all too brief, in my mind. But as I started into my line I took note of who was watching. And it was a lot of people, more people than had ever before heard me say anything. I froze. I froze in my one line. Ten minutes earlier, Danny McIlroy recited his part like a Shakespearean actor, and here I was stumbling on the fourth word of a sixteen-word part. Mr. Gillespie finally fed me my line, and I stumbled along. My one big chance to stand before that great church audience and display my theatrical talent, and I blew it. The audience undid me.

Let's think about your audience. It is, I suspect, what Jesus is wanting to get to in Matthew 6 and this part of the Sermon on the Mount. "Beware," Jesus says, "of practicing your piety before others in order to be seen by them." "To be seen" in Greek is the word *theathenai*, from which we get our word *theater*. Beware, Jesus says, of what your theater is. Beware of your audience.

I want to think with you about your audience. What audience are you playing to? Who is occupying your theater?

My guess is that, if we were honest, most of us would say that there is not simply one audience before whom we perform our lives. Each of us has several audiences that we are playing to, wouldn't you say? For many if not all of us, our lives are played out on one of those rotating stages that circle several galleries of people before us. At one point, for example, we are performing in front of our employer or work associates. We act in a certain way as to engender the favorable response of those who sign our checks and give us our bonuses. Rotate the stage, and we are now performing in front of our families: our parents, children, siblings, and spouse. They are watching us act our familial part, and we hope beyond hope that they are satisfied with our performance. Rotate the stage again, and now we are acting in front of our neighbors, friends, and community. These people maybe don't know us real well, but we sure want them to see us in a certain light and performing a certain part. Rotate the stage another time, and now we are enacting a role before our church family. They are looking to see how well we undertake our discipleship part. Rotate the stage once again, and we are performing before total strangers, people to whom we give little thought as to what they think of how we act.

"All the world's a stage," Shakespeare wrote, "and all the men and women merely players; They have their exits and entrances; and one man in his time plays many parts."

Behavioral psychologists would tell you that a whole and integrated person stays in character while rotating on the stage—that the same character and the same lines are being recited before the work crowd and the family audience and the friends' group and the church family and the assorted strangers. To put it another way, a whole and integrated person could put all those audiences into one theater and not skip a beat or lose track of a line while staring into that collection of her life's audience. It's called self-control, knowing oneself and having control of oneself while upon the shifting stage.

How would that be for you? How would it be to take all the audiences of your life and put them into one theater with all eyes staring upon you as you enact your role as a human being? Imagine your child sitting next to your boss, sitting next to your golf partner, sitting next to your next-door neighbor, sitting next to your parent, sitting next to your brother and sister in Christ, sitting next to the stranger on the highway who just cut you off. How would that be for you? Do you know yourself? Are you true to yourself while in the theater?

For most of us there might be some level of crisis that would arise when forced to play before our several audiences at one time. It's like going to someone's funeral and saying to yourself on the way out, *Boy, I didn't know all those things about Joe.* Strange how you don't realize all the theaters a person is playing to. Would there be any surprises for anyone in your life when they came to your funeral and listened to your eulogy?

"Beware," Jesus says, "beware of your theater. Beware of the audience you're playing to."

Truth is, it may not only be overwhelming to consider bringing all of our audiences together and playing a consistent role in front of them. It may be, according to Jesus, the very last thing we should be thinking about. The truth is that each of our audiences demands something different from us. Underscore the word "demand." For any actor, the audience becomes the master. The audience judges the performance, and the scales of judgment are different in each theater. The expectations of behavior are different. We rise and fall according to the demands of the audience.

So it should be no surprise that when Jesus starts his teaching on theater in Matthew 6, he quickly steers us to think not of many audiences and many theaters but of only one audience and only one person in the theater.

"When you pray . . . go into your room and shut the door and pray to your Father who sees in secret."

"When you give alms, do not let your left hand know what your right hand is doing, so that your alms may be done in secret."

"When you fast, put oil on your head and wash your face, so that your fasting may not be seen by others but by your Father who is in secret."

Do you see what Jesus is doing? He's emptying out the theater. He is asking your boss, your family, your friends, your neighbors, and all the strangers to leave. He is clearing out the theater and asking only one person to remain inside the theater of your life and mine. "No one can serve two masters; for a slave will either hate the one and love the other, or be devoted to the one and despise the other." Jesus is trying to simplify our lives. He is trying to shrink our audience down to one.

Who are you playing to? It may be the plainest, simplest, and yet most profound question of your life.

We've already talked about some of the audiences: Employer, family, friends, brothers and sisters in Christ, strangers. But the list could go on. Maybe you're playing to a person in your past, to a person of influence, or to a dysfunctional family system. Maybe you're playing to your financial advisor, or perhaps to a teacher or a coach.

When I was in seminary we had two required semesters of preaching—one of which was a practicum wherein you preached before an audience of your peers and two faculty members. Following your preaching, you were then before your peers and critiqued by both of the faculty members. Talk about an audience! So I wrote and I preached my very first sermon there at Princeton, and the professor stood up after I was done and before my peers and friends proceeded to say that that was one of the worst sermons he had ever heard preached from the Christian pulpit. He was a very affirming guy. I would be less than honest if I did not tell you that even today he is someone I still play to . . . someone I still preach to.

What about you? Who are you playing to?

It is no coincidence that in Matthew 6, just after Jesus spends a long time talking about all these audiences we play to, he turns to the subject of worry. "Do not worry about your life," he says. And I suppose the reason he says it is that he knows there is only one audience in this life that matters: the audience that's left after we have emptied out the theater. It's the audience of one. And it may be that so much of the worry of our lives has to do with all these theaters and audiences. Keeping up with the Joneses, pleasing the boss, making sure our kids have everything (I mean *everything*), putting on appearances in front of neighbors and strangers—all these selves we try to be. Jesus says, "Do not worry. . . . Strive first for the kingdom of God and his righteousness . . . and all these things will be given to you." Play out your life before an audience of one. Be yourself.

Remember that haunting line at the end of *Death of a Salesman* when the family of Willy Loman is gathered at his grave? Willy has lived a salesman's life, going from account to account, deal to deal . . . trying to make something of himself. He's disappointed all the important people in his life . . . most of all himself. He meets a tragic death, and his son Biff stands over the grave and says, "He never knew who he was."

So the young rabbi makes his journey to the cross. And while the disciples watch—along with the Pharisees, the Sadducees, the chief priests, the crowds, and the Romans—Jesus seems rather oblivious to it all because he's playing to a theater of one. In the Garden of Gethsemane he's talking just to one. And on the cross the conversation is just with one. It's the only audience he has. It's the only way he will end up doing the right thing.

Self-control is the fruit Paul saved for the last on his list. I don't suspect it was for any rhyme or reason. But upon further reflection, maybe he saved the best for last. For without the self—knowledge of the self and control of the self—how could we ever hope to love, to be joyful, to have peace, to be patient, kind, good, faithful, and gentle? Without the self—to know who we are and whose we are—do we stand much chance to bear such fruit, to follow the one who was there at our beginning and will be there at our end, and who in between gives his life for us? This is our audience, isn't it? The one who gives us our life and his life, too. This is our audience.

And there he sits, the only one in the theater, and says, "Be yourself. Recite your line. Play your part."

Walt Whitman wrote,

> O me! O life! . . . of the questions of these recurring;
> Of the endless trains of the faithless—of cities fill'd with the foolish;
> Of myself forever reproaching myself, (for who more foolish than I, and who more faithless?)
> Of eyes that vainly crave the light—of the objects mean—of the struggle ever renew'd;
> Of the poor results of all—of the plodding and sordid crowds I see around me;

Of the empty and useless years of the rest—with
the rest me intertwined;
The question, O me! so sad, recurring—What
good amid these, O me, O life?

Answer.

That you are here—that life exists, and identity;
That the powerful play goes on, and you will con-
tribute a verse.

CHAPTER 11

When Do You Give Up?

—⁓—

Luke 22:54–62; James 5:7–11

THE COMIC STRIP THAT MOST of us woke up to for many years was *Peanuts*, Charles Schulz's depiction of young children trying to figure out the world and themselves. Its main character is Charlie Brown, who spends most of his life pretty discouraged. Life, for the most part, does not go well for Charlie Brown. If something can go wrong, it does. If he flies a kite, it ends up in a tree. If he has a crush on the little redheaded girl, it remains unrequited. If he is pitching for his baseball team, they lose by historic margins. And about once a year, usually in the fall as I remember, the Sunday comic strip would feature the classic test of personalities between Lucy and Charlie Brown, when Lucy offers to hold the football for Charlie Brown so that he can kick it. Now as soon as you read the first panel of this strip, you knew how it was going to end: Charlie Brown on his back, having had the football pulled away by dear Lucy. As far as I know, it never turned out any other way. And it always starts out the same way—with Lucy promising and assuring and providing some evidence of her good faith—and Charlie Brown taking the bait and then *Wham!* In one strip Lucy even offers a written and supposedly binding contract—a signed document—that promises she will not pull away the football. Charlie Brown thinks he has an ironclad commitment, only to find out that the document had not been notarized.

Every time that strip appeared, we were left to wonder: Who is Charlie Brown really? Is he a chump? Is he just one of those losers who never gets it, who allows the world to roll over him and chew him up and spit him out? Is he one of those naïve characters who doesn't quite get the real world? Or—to the contrary—is Charlie Brown one of those endangered species that just doesn't want to give up? Perhaps he doesn't want to give up on the world, he doesn't want to give up on his friends, he doesn't want to give up on Lucy. As long and as often as the kite ends up in the tree, the mailbox stays empty of love notes from the redheaded girl, and the football keeps getting pulled away, Charlie Brown never lets go of the remaining ounces of hope that maybe, just maybe, things will be different next time.

You might think the same way of a Chicago Cubs fan. The Chicago Cubs have not won a World Series for over a century (as of this writing). Five generations have come and gone, and the Cubs have not brought home the World Series trophy. We may have in fact come to that moment in history where no true Chicago Cubs fan alive today can say that the Cubs have won a championship during his or her lifetime. That's amazing—the longest championship drought of a professional team on the North American continent. And yet, on any given day at Wrigley Field, thirty thousand to forty thousand fans show up at the Friendly Confines to hope beyond hope that this may be the year. Every September they say, "Maybe next year," and every April they say, "Maybe this year." Are these Cubs fans chumps? Or do they embody what is best about the spirit—staying with your team through thick and thin . . . or should we say just "thin"?

No one wants to be a chump. No one wants to be accused of hanging in there too long.

I actually once threw out the question on Facebook and asked for comments: At what point, I asked, do we give up on each other? To my surprise I got about twenty responses, and they were all over the map and all along the spectrum between the fear of being taken advantage of and the need to protect oneself—and the unconditional love and everlasting hope that keep us from never letting go.

Chumpness to never-ending hope.

Maybe that is what was on Peter's mind when he asked Jesus, on the topic of forgiveness, "How many times must I forgive?" And so as to calculate the limit between grace, hope, and chumpness, Peter throws out his most aggressive guess: "Seven times? Is that enough? Does that satisfy the heart of God?" And Jesus says, "Seven times, all right. Seven times seventy?" Now the mathematicians hear in that answer 490, but that's not Jesus' point. It is his hyperbolic way of saying that chumpness is part of the game. It is his way of steering the interpretation of the law away from an eye for an eye and a tooth for a tooth. In the Sermon on the Mount, Jesus says that if someone asks you to walk with him a mile, walk with him two. If someone slaps you on one cheek, turn to him the other. If someone sues you for your coat, give him your cloak as well. Boy, talk about being a chump.

The truth is that none of us has it on the inside to do those things, do we? We really don't have it inside us to turn the other cheek, to walk that extra mile, to forgive seven times seventy. It's not the way we are wired. No one wants to be a chump. Fool me once, shame on you. Fool me twice, shame on me.

Maybe that's why the apostle, when he comes up with his fruit of the Spirit, was sure to include the fruit of patience. These are not fruit of human strength, will, and capacity; these are fruit of *the Spirit*. And if anything stretches far past human strength, will, and capacity, it is this gift of patience. If anything demands the work of the Spirit in us, it is this art of patience. When we are at that point of saying I have walked too far, I have forgiven too many times, I have turned the cheek too often, only the Spirit working in us could cause us to go yet another measure, to find at least some creative way to not give up, to say that somehow someway—whether we keep distance or hold close—we will not give up on each other.

Makrothumia is the Greek word that Paul uses for *patience*. The Greek would say it this way: long-suffering. The fruit of the Spirit is long-suffering. How long is long? Peter asks. Jesus says long. How long do we walk, and Jesus says long. How long do we keep giving away, and Jesus says long. Long-suffering sure is not something we are wired to do either, is it? Suffer. Suffer long with the other. Paul says, I want to know Christ in his sufferings. And if there was anyone who suffered with another, it was the man nailed up on a cross, saying, "Father, forgive them, for they don't know what they are doing." And those to whom he was extending this grace even in his death, what were they saying? "Chump."

Perhaps not Peter, the one who went as far as the courtyard on that fateful day, but it was as far as he could go. Three times he was given the chance to keep walking alongside the Savior and three times he denied—only to receive Christ's icy stare. Oh, we can only imagine that what Peter had to say was, "Please. Please be patient. Please suffer with me. Please forgive me . . . for I don't know what I'm doing either."

Paul, too, learns it the hard way. Remember the story of Paul and Barnabas and Mark, who had been the original missionary team for the early church, traveling to bring the good news of Christ beyond Palestine. But in that first trip Mark bailed from the team. He wasn't up to it. He went home and left Paul and Barnabas to do the heavy lifting. So when trip number two came around, it was Paul and Barnabas, but now Mark wants a second chance, wanting Paul and Barnabas to take the chance. And Paul says, "Nuh-uh." Fool me once, shame on you. Fool me twice, shame on me. Sorry, pal, you had the chance. You blew it. And Barnabas says, "Whoa, what about this patience thing?" And so probably in words he would someday come to regret, Paul says, "My patience can only go so far." And so they split. Paul went one way, and Barnabas along with Mark went the other way. We don't know if Paul and Barnabas ever got back together again.

But what the record does show—as far as we can tell—is that Paul and Mark did get back together again. In his last imprisonment Paul writes to Timothy and implores him to bring to him that one on whom he once gave up. "Get Mark and bring him with you, for he is useful in my ministry."

At what point do we give up on each other? And to my Facebook question, one of my friends responded with the answer perhaps all of us would give. Said he, "At what point do we give up on each other? Jesus' answer would probably be never. Mine would be somewhat less."

Amen to that.

Yet still the call of grace echoes in our ears: forgive us our debts, the Savior taught us to pray, *as* we forgive our debtors.

George Eliot, in her wonderful novel *Adam Bede*, put it this way:

> These fellow mortals, every one, must be accepted as they are: you can neither straighten their noses nor brighten their wit nor rectify their dispositions; and it is these people—amongst whom your life is passed—that it is needful you should tolerate, pity, and love: it is these more or less ugly, stupid, inconsistent people whose movement of goodness you should be able to admire—for whom you should cherish all possible hopes, all possible patience.

Such is the difficult road of following the long-suffering Messiah. Always room between what he would do and what we want to do. And in between—the fruit of the Spirit.

CHAPTER 12

Catching Your Second Wind

—∞—

Ezekiel 37:1–10; Acts 2:1–4

WHEN I WAS IN JUNIOR high school, I ran track. The event I ran was the 880—the half-mile. Today they call it the 800 meters. Back then, way back in 1972, there was a collegiate runner who also ran the half-mile. His name was Dave Wottle. Some of you may remember him. Dave Wottle was my hero. He was famous for two things. First was his headgear. You usually don't think of headgear when you think of track, but Dave Wottle wore a hat when he ran. An old golf hat. You always knew where Dave Wottle was in the race because you could see his hat. The other thing Dave Wottle was famous for was his kick. People called it the Dave Wottle kick. A "kick" in track is the extra burst of speed a runner puts on, if he or she has it to put on, at the end of the race—that last sprint to the finish line. Dave Wottle's style was that, throughout the first two-thirds of the race, he would languish at the end of the pack. You would watch this man in the golf cap get farther and farther behind. And halfway through the second lap of this two-lap race, you would be convinced that there was no way that Dave Wottle had it in him to catch the leaders. But then all of a sudden you began to see the kick, as if the man in the golf cap was catching his second wind. And before you knew it he would begin to pass one guy after the other, and within 200 yards of the finish he would often pass as many as ten guys until all of sudden he would be neck and neck with the leader. He won the gold medal in the 1972 Olympics just that way. The famous Dave Wottle kick. The amazing thing about Dave Wottle is that when he ran, he almost always ran the second lap faster than the first. He always seemed to get a second wind, and the second wind is what seemed to carry him to the finish line.

The second lap faster than the first.

Life doesn't often work that way, does it? Usually the first lap is the fastest. You start out young . . . you have energy . . . you're indestructible. You're racing around that first lap pretty fast. But then the years add up and your body starts to give way a little. You get tired. The second lap gets a little tougher and the pace gets a little slower. It happens that way in careers sometimes, too. You come out of school with the freshest ideas and the willingness to work the longest hours. You rise up the ladder pretty quickly, and you are racing around that first lap. But then comes the second lap, and all of a sudden you see people passing you. You wonder if you can keep up. And then you learn that they might not even want you around for the second lap. The world doesn't really much believe in the second lap because the world doesn't understand much about the second wind.

It's what I love about the Bible. The Bible believes in the second wind. The Bible is filled with stories about people getting their second winds and running their second laps faster than their first. Abraham and Sarah, an old man and woman finishing their first lap in the land of Ur, were likely preparing for a slow second lap, but then they got their second wind—and they were off to the land of Canaan, having a baby at age ninety and becoming the father and mother of many nations. Their second lap went even farther than their first. Moses had a pretty good first lap as the heir apparent to the pharaoh of Egypt. But then he ends up out in the wilderness—literally, it seems, out to pasture. Then came the second wind. The burning bush. The call to go back and deliver the people of Israel. The second lap awaited him, and the second lap was a whole lot faster. He caught his second wind.

What a glorious first lap the people of Israel had run. The great judges and kings of their past—Joshua and Deborah and David and Solomon . . . it's hard to run a better first lap than that. But then because of their disobedience they are taken into exile, taken away from their home, captive in a foreign land. And Ezekiel the prophet calls out to them and says that when he looks upon the people of Israel, all he sees is a valley of dry bones. The people of Israel do not believe that they can have a new life. They have run in their own minds what they think is the end of the race. No second lap. But then God says to Ezekiel, “Prophesy—prophesy! Tell them about the wind.” In Hebrew the word is *ruach*, and it means *wind* or *breath* or *spirit*. “Tell them,” God says to Ezekiel, “tell them about the second wind. Tell them about the breath of God that can raise up the valley of dry bones and make it live again, so that they can run the second lap faster than the first.” And sure enough, the people of Israel come home from their exile and rebuild again, and they prepare for the coming Messiah.

And what about the disciples? Can you have a better first lap than them? Three years with Jesus, learning from his teaching, given power to cast out demons and heal people, personal encounters with the resurrected Christ. You couldn’t ask for a better first lap. So they come to Jesus and say, “Is the race over? Aren’t we all through?” And Jesus says, “You have another lap.” “Another lap?” they say. Jesus says, “Another lap. But guess what? You get a second wind. And if you can believe it, the second wind will give you power to do far beyond what you could have thought about doing up until now.” And so Jesus says, “Wait, wait for the second wind. Because when the second wind comes, the Holy Spirit, you are going to turn the world upside down.” And that’s what happened. The world got turned upside down.

I’m not sure where you are in the race. You might be just out of the blocks. You might be having an incredible first lap. You might be slowing down on the second lap. You might feel like you’re not even being given a chance to run the second lap, but do you know what today is? Today is the day of the second wind. Do you know what tomorrow is? Tomorrow is the day of the second wind. The day after? The day after is the day of the second wind. You see, we are living in the era of the second wind. We are living in the time when God is seeking to pour out his spirit upon all people. God has this second wind for all our second laps. God says to us, "It doesn't matter how good or bad your first lap was. It's time to catch your second wind, and let me fill you and use you and have you do far more abundantly than you could ever ask or think."

Dave Wottle's story has a second part. Several years ago I also mentioned in one of my sermons my interest in and inspiration from Dave Wottle. When church was over, I put the sermon away and forgot about it. About three or four months later I received in the mail a large envelope from Rhodes College in Tennessee, and I almost threw it away because pastors get lots of marketing stuff from colleges. But by grace I opened it up and found a handwritten note on Rhodes College stationery from the director of admissions. The note read,

> Dear Pastor McConnell,
> My son Mike, who was a computer science major in college and is always surfing the Internet it seems, came across your sermon "Catching Your Second Wind." I was flattered to be mentioned in your sermon. It's ironic that my pastor at Germantown Methodist Church made reference to the Olympic race last month in a sermon he delivered.

> Having been an 880 runner yourself, I thought you might enjoy the enclosed photo. Your new church facility looks beautiful and it's obvious your church family is being used by God to successfully spread the gospel of Christ.
>
> Sincerely,
> Dave Wottle

He signed the picture, "Steve—Best wishes as you continue to spread the Gospel of Christ."

Now you cannot begin to imagine how thrilled I was to receive a letter and a signed picture of my number-one track hero of all time. But I tell you the second half of the story for two reasons. First, Dave Wottle had a second chapter to his life, maybe more than that, he would say. He won the gold medal at age twenty-two. He did not compete in the Olympics before or after. You can argue, perhaps, that there couldn't be a much better first lap than that—winning the gold medal. Everything is downhill from there. But I am guessing, and it's only a guess, that Dave Wottle would say, at the end of the day, his thirty-plus years of working in higher education and affecting the lives of thousands and thousands of college students, raising his own children, loving his wife, and being a good member at the Germantown Methodist Church is a better lap. He got his second wind. Find yourself a copy of *Chariots of Fire*—the movie about Eric Liddell, the 1924 Scottish Olympic gold medalist. Fastest man in the world. What was his second lap after the Olympics? Missionary to China. Which lap was the better lap?

The second reason I share that letter with you is that when that second wind fills you and moves you and inspires you, it usually means you have someone in particular to touch—someone who can receive a blessing from you. Dave Wottle didn't have to write that letter. He didn't have to take the time to handwrite a note and sign a picture and send it to a complete stranger. No one would have known had he chosen not to, and no one would have thought the lesser of him. But he did it. Maybe it might be a blessing. Maybe it might be an encouragement. Maybe it might be a little boost along the way. So from person to person, the second wind—dare we call it that?—blew. One brother in Christ blessed by another brother in Christ.

I have an old friend whose father for over sixty years was a giant of a pastor. He was a great churchman, a college president, and a great preacher. He served the church faithfully for all those years, but the last chapter of his life was a struggle. He suffered a couple of heart attacks and grew very weak. He spent most of his time at home and was disappointed not to be as active as he once had been. Finally, it came time for him to go to the hospital, where he knew he would die in a few days. His daughter struggled with why he had to suffer so and why was it taking so long, as she put it, for the Lord to take him home? The day before he died, he received a visit from the newly ordained pastor at the church he had been attending. Pretty wet behind the ears, and somewhat intimidated by this giant of a man, the young pastor visited with him for a bit and then prayed. When the prayer was over, the great preacher kept holding his hand. He pulled the young man close and then whispered to him, "You are a great pastor." That's all he said, but that's all he needed to say. It's all the young man needed to hear from the great giant. A blessing. It was the movement of the second wind.

We who live in the season of Pentecost live with the promise that at whatever time, whatever stage, whatever age—no matter how well the first lap has gone—the promise is that the second lap may have something even greater. We just need to catch our second wind. As long as we have breath, there will always be another breath—*ruach*—blessing us, that we may be a blessing.

CHAPTER 13

Let's Be Honest

—⁓—

John 20:19–29

When I was growing up, I had a classmate I'll call Richard. He was a pretty smart guy. Some would say he was too smart for his own good. And the reason they would have said it—and I have to admit that I was one of them from time to time—was that Richard was that guy in the class who always felt compelled to ask a question. After the teacher had done her best to explain the subject at hand—a math equation, a science problem, an act of Congress, a classic poem—and while most of us were robotically taking our notes and hoping to extract the bare minimum out of our class time (i.e., what was going to be on the test), our friend Richard's hand invariably would shoot up with a question. At that point, most of us would roll our eyes and murmur to each other, "Geez, why does he have to ask so many questions?" Truth is, about half the time that Richard asked a question, we were very glad for it—because it was a question we all had but worried that the question was dumb and we didn't want to look stupid asking it. But Richard would ask, and we were usually grateful for the answer. Yet that did not keep us from a certain level of impatience when it came to Richard's continued query.

We all have, I suspect, a certain threshold for questions.

How many of us have been subjected to the classic line of questioning from a three-year-old? Daddy, where does a leaf come from? The leaf comes from a tree. And where does the tree come from? The tree comes from a seed. And where does the seed come from? The seed comes from God. And where does God come from? I don't know; go ask your mother.

We all have a certain threshold for questions.

Some of us may remember the old detective series *Columbo* starring Peter Falk—the frumpy, unkempt detective whose appearance suggested a certain lack of sophistication and smarts, except that he kept asking questions. Stupid, persistent questions that tried the patience of the guilty and nonguilty. Why, why, why do you want to know these things? It was all part of the puzzle.

Galileo, the seventeenth-century astronomer, pointed his telescope to the night sky and wondered, along with his predecessor, Copernicus: Is it possible that the universe is not geocentric? Is it possible that the earth revolves around the sun instead of the sun revolving around the earth? It was a destabilizing question, especially for the church. The question threw too many other things up for grabs. But there Galileo sat in the back of the class with his hand straight up, begging to ask his question. And the answer was, *no*, you can't ask the question.

They put him under house arrest eventually and condemned his science to heresy.

We have a certain threshold when it comes to questions.

So in John's Gospel we find Thomas in the back of the classroom amid his fellow pupils—Peter, James, John, and the like—and everybody seems to get this answer of the resurrection, except for brother Thomas. He has his hand in the air. He had missed the class when Jesus arrived and spoke and dispersed the Holy Spirit. He was absent that day. All he knew was that now a rather strange rumor was going around the classroom that the dead rabbi was alive, that he appeared and spoke and he came and went without benefit of a door or window. Up went Thomas's hand. It wasn't the first time he was calling something into question. A couple of weeks before—when the rabbi's whole mission seemed to be on a suicide course, with Jesus insisting on traveling into the hostile territory of Jerusalem—Thomas piped up, expressing his doubt and saying in essence, "I don't like where this is going, but one for all and all for one. Let us go with the rabbi, and if one dies, we all die."

Then, in the waning hours before the cross, Jesus has the disciples together in the upper room and tries to teach them about the Father's house with many rooms and that he goes to prepare a place for them. This is the way he must go. Did they understand? Up goes Thomas's hand. "Uh, no, actually. I don't understand. And if these other guys were honest, they'd say the same thing. They'd have their hands up, too—if they were courageous enough to ask what might sound like a stupid question. Lord, we don't know where you are going."

Here they are after the crucifixion and burial, and there are ten votes on the jury for the appearance of the risen Jesus—and one vote still in doubt. “Unless I see the evidence, unless I see the punctured hands and pierced side, I will not believe.” Ten to one. Hung jury. Mistrial. Where do we go from here?

Then the Gospel writer follows with this next sentence: “A week later his disciples were again in the house and Thomas was with them.” Thomas the questioner. Thomas the doubter. Thomas, who wouldn’t take their word for it. Thomas, who just couldn’t be happy accepting what everyone else has said. We are told that he was with them. There was still room for Thomas, his questions, and his doubt. A week later his disciples were again in the house, and Thomas was with them.

Not unlike that time, I suppose, when the twelve of them were out on the water and the wind was kicking and the waves were beating—and here comes Jesus, walking on the water. This time Peter raised his hand and said, “Question! If it’s you, bid me to come to you on the water.” And Jesus said, “Come.” And so Peter with all his certainty comes. But the truth is that it’s not all certainty that Peter has. He has some uncertainty, some questions still to be answered, some doubts about these troughs of water lapping at his feet. Sure enough, the uncertainty has him sinking. Now Peter really has his hand in the air. “Save me!” The Gospel writer tells us that then Jesus caught him with his hand in the air and said, “You’re not as certain as you thought you were, are you? That’s OK. Get in the boat and join the rest of them.” And so there in the boat sits Peter dripping wet—but there was room for the soggy disciple with his doubt and uncertainty.

We are not saved by our certainty, are we? We are saved by grace. If those disciples understood anything, it was that. Lord knows they made a habit of getting a lot of things wrong along the way. Theirs was a course of mishaps and misunderstandings—two steps forward and three steps back. They understood that desperate father when he said to Jesus, "Lord, I believe. Help my unbelief!" And if there was any one of them who didn't understand it—who somehow got it in his head that his certainty would win the day—it was the one who was not in that room that day when Jesus appeared again: Judas, the certain one, so certain that his way was the right way.

"It's by grace we are saved." Who wrote those words? The once-certain man—the apostle Paul. No room for doubt for this guy, so certain that they're wrong and he's right that it didn't take much to cross the line to the stoning of Stephen and the arrest and murder of those early Christians. Certainty can get you into a lot of trouble, you know. Oh no, Paul says, after getting knocked off his horse by the resurrected Christ, raising his hand to shield the blinding light—and the risen Christ reaches down and saves him from his blinded sinking. Oh no, Paul says. We are saved by grace and not by our certainty.

Many argue, for myriad different reasons, that Abraham Lincoln was our greatest president. Most would point to his unrelenting pursuit of the abolition of slavery as one of his greatest gifts to the country, though it came at the cost of hundreds of thousands of lives. Yet even throughout the war, Lincoln still expressed to himself—and aloud to others—the doubts of his being right. At one point he found himself speaking to Orville Hickman Browning, senator from Illinois, who was applauding the president for his forthright stand against slavery, to which Lincoln replied, "Suppose, though, God is against us in our view on the subject of slavery in this country, and our method of dealing with it?" Browning was shocked to hear the president's question and was awed to see how even then the president was thinking deeply of what a higher power than man sought to bring about by the great events then transpiring.

By grace we are saved, not by our certainty.

So that first community of Christ assembles, resisting the temptation to shrink their number through some false sense of certainty; the disciples make sure that Thomas is included in their fellowship. For none of them, frankly, deserve to be there. They have all stumbled and fallen to this place. But together through their shared conviction and uncertainty they wait for the Risen One to appear in his grace, to take their risen hands and pull them from their fears.

We are a mixed-up bunch, aren't we? We who sit in these pews, who claim membership in the church, who take on the banner of a particular spiritual tradition, who embrace the identity of Christian. Mixed-up, to be sure. Thank the good Lord that he does not demand of any of us a doubt-free life in order to come to his table. Thank the good Lord that raised hands are welcome here. Thank the good Lord that if anything is required, it's that we're honest—with the One who invites, with those who are invited, and with ourselves. Lest we forget that when those first twelve gathered at table with bread and cup, they were surprised to hear that one among them was soon to betray Jesus. And soon around him were twelve raised hands. Twelve hands with twelve voices that asked with great uncertainty, "Is it I, Lord?"

Were they just being honest with themselves?

By grace we are saved.

CHAPTER 14

Sticking to Your Story

—ᨓ—

John 21:1–19

MAYBE YOU'VE HEARD THE STORY of the four college sophomores who, instead of spending the weekend studying for their American history final, decided to go on a little ski weekend in the mountains. Upon their return and realizing they were not at all prepared to take their final, they went to the professor and told him that the night before they had gotten a flat tire and the time that it took to get it fixed kept them from studying for the test. Would it be possible to take the test the next day so that they could have time to study? The professor thought about it for a moment and then graciously said that he understood. Sure, they could take the test the next day. The next day the four students arrived, and the professor sat them in the four corners of the room. He gave them the test, which came in two parts—two questions. On the first page was the first question, worth five points: Who was the first American president? *Wow*, they thought, *this test is going to be pretty easy.*

They turned to the second page and read the second question, worth ninety-five points: Which tire?

Perhaps the most important thing in sticking to your story is knowing your story to begin with.

John tells us a story that begins with a few men fishing. I am not a fisherman. I have fished in my life, but I have no fish stories, except for "no fish" stories. I can very much relate to our friends in the story John spins. A subset of the disciples has gone out onto the Sea of Galilee. They are doing some night fishing and having no luck. They're catching nothing. They're dragging their nets, but the fish are smarter than they are.

As the story goes, the sun begins to rise, and they look to the shore and see the figure of a man. The man directs them to cast their nets to the other side of the boat. "Excuse me? Been there, done that. Just there a couple minutes ago. What*ever*." Maybe to humor the man more than anything else, they throw their nets to the other side and catch almost more than they can handle. Something is up here, and this something helps them to recognize Jesus.

So they go paddling to shore, and when they get there they bring their catch of fish—a catch, mind you, that Jesus had directed them to—and there Jesus is, cooking five loaves and two fish and inviting them to bring some of the fish they had caught. This is one of the first marks of the resurrected life—hearing and responding to the invitation to give to Christ what he has already given to us. "Bring some of the fish you caught." Isn't it interesting how Jesus—knowing that without him they wouldn't have caught a blessed thing—dignifies their participation, honors the part they had to play, and says, "Bring some of the fish *you* caught." He invites them to freely give what he had helped them to procure. Hopefully the irony and the truth have not been lost on these disciples. One of the great challenges of living the resurrected life is to remember that whatever we have has been given to us. We really can claim no ownership.

My grandfather used to say that the perfect illustration of original sin was to put two two-year-olds into one room with one toy. Sooner or later you are going to hear the word, "mine." From an early age we have this uncanny knack of forgetting that whatever we have has come from someone else. It's hard to share when the first word that comes to mind is "mine." We so detest "mine" when it comes from the mouth of a two-year-old, but when it comes from someone who is thirty-two, fifty-two, or seventy-two, we kind of expect it: my house, my property, my money, my car. "Bring some of the fish you caught." God graces us with the joy of participating in the catch, but the truth is that he was the one who pointed out the fish. One of the greatest graces God gives us is when we see that everything we have is not "mine," it's God's. And so it is better to hear Jesus say, "Bring some of the fish I caught through you." That's where the joy is.

The conversation shifts after this breakfast of bread and fish—a meal they first saw in the feeding of the five thousand. The resurrected Christ pulls Peter aside for a little one-on-one conversation. At some point the encounter with the resurrected Christ becomes an individual one. On Easter Sunday recently we had a group encounter with the resurrected Christ. Together with three thousand of our closest friends we gathered at the empty tomb and rejoiced that he is not here; he is risen. We came and left en masse. But there comes a time when the resurrected Christ pulls us from the body of believers and asks for a one-on-one. Dietrich Bonhoeffer, in his book *The Cost of Discipleship*, said, "Through the call of Jesus [people] become individuals. . . . It is no choice of their own that makes them individuals: it is Christ who makes them individuals by calling them." So Jesus makes Peter an individual by pulling him aside and having what turns out to be a hard exchange.

Now, you and I don't like the thought of having a hard conversation with Jesus. Frankly, most of us would avoid it at any cost. We don't want the subject to be about us—at least if Jesus were suggesting any changes. If there is any conversation we like to have with Jesus, it's usually a conversation about someone else. You know what I mean. I'm guessing that about 90 percent of the pastoral conversations I have with people are about someone else. People want to talk to me about this person and that person—their spouse, this or that group of people, their children, their friends. It's not an uncommon remark for a preacher to hear from someone going out the door, "Nice sermon, pastor. I just wish my [husband/daughter/boss] was here to hear it." We so much want the subject to be about someone else.

One of the great lessons I learned from C. S. Lewis is that the only person's story you are ever going to have any chance of understanding is your own, and even our own story is pretty complicated. There are still so many things I don't understand about myself, and I have been living with me for over fifty-five years. If you've got you figured out, then you are one of the great exceptions to the human race. But how often I want to turn the conversation with Jesus to someone else, about how good or how bad someone else is! And yet, writes C. S. Lewis,

> What can you ever really know of other people's souls—of their temptations, their opportunities, their struggles? One soul in the whole creation you do know: and it is the only one whose fate is placed in your hands. If there is a God, you are, in a sense, alone with Him. You cannot put Him off with speculations about your next-door neighbors or memories of what you have read in books. What will all that chat and hearsay count (will you even be able to remember it?) when the anesthetic fog which we call "nature" or "the real world" fades away and the Presence in which you have always stood becomes palpable, immediate, and unavoidable?

So for Peter there came the time when the resurrected Christ pulled him aside and had what we might call the first "come-to-Jesus meeting," which began with a question: "Simon, son of John, do you love me more than these?" Lots of scholars have lots of opinions about whom Jesus is talking about when it comes "these." I tend to think that Jesus is talking about the fish. "Simon, son of John, do you love me more than those fish you were just trying to catch?" In other words, "Simon, son of John, it's a new day. All night you were back in the old life of trying to catch fish and make a living and do whatever it is you'd like to do, but now the question is, 'Do you love me more than these?' Do you understand that the resurrection life is an invitation into a new chapter in which you get to put your life up against the calling of God?"

"Yes, Lord, you know that I love you."

Then, Jesus says, "I have a new work for you: Tend my sheep. I'm changing your job description from fisherman to shepherd. The resurrected life is expanding in you, Peter, and now I am inviting you into a new work. Tend my sheep. I am the good shepherd, so I invite you now into this work with me." Now, all of a sudden, our friend Peter has some soul-searching to do. Take care of my people, Jesus says. I am leaving you this responsibility. And now Peter has to tend to his own story. What is the next thing God is calling me to be in this ever-expanding life of resurrection?

But then the question comes again. "Simon, son of John, do you love me?"

Whoa, whoa, whoa—I thought I just answered that question. "Yes, Lord, you know that I love you."

"Feed my lambs," Jesus says, as if to remind Peter that the new life is not simply about getting an answer right. "Love" is an easy word to throw around.

"Do you love me?" he asks for a third time, and by now Peter takes a little umbrage.

Hey, I answered the question, didn't I? Isn't that enough?

And Jesus says, "We'll see if it is enough, because the resurrection life is more than just showing up on the beach and seeing Jesus and saying, 'Isn't that great!'" The resurrected life is the joy and the challenge of expansion whereby we live into the new job description.

And that's what we see, isn't it? Story after story in the Acts of the Apostles show Peter trying to live into the new job description. And he had no idea how big it was going to be, but with each and every step we see Peter taking responsibility for the resurrected life.

He takes responsibility for picking new church leadership.

He takes responsibility to interpret to the people what in heaven's name had just happened to them at Pentecost.

He takes responsibility to preach the good news of resurrection to a crowd that had every potential to be as against him as for him.

He takes responsibility for the lame man outside the temple: "Silver and gold have I none, but I give you what I have, in the name of Jesus Christ, stand up and walk."

He takes responsibility for the vision that came that maybe, just maybe, the gospel wasn't just for the Jews. Maybe, just maybe, God is bigger than that. Maybe the dream is that all people will be included in the grace of God—and maybe my job is to make that happen.

It's amazing what happens when Jesus pulls you out of a crowd and says, "What's it going to be?" Enough talk about the church and the gospel and the mission. Now it's the will of God for you and me to have a hard conversation, a come-to-Jesus meeting, a time when you get to wonder about the expanding life of resurrection within you. Now's the time to consider a change of job description. Have you considered that recently? Have you wondered in what new way you are going to take responsibility for the resurrected life? Or are you already starting to whittle away this resurrected life so that it can fit into what you've always been doing? Will there be any evidence to convict you that you also were a witness to the empty tomb?

You might at first see no evidence of such witness if writer Anne Lamott were to walk into the room. She doesn't look like most of us; her dreadlocks would stand out. She doesn't talk like most of us; her language, shall we say, is a little earthy. Her faith may not necessarily fit comfortably into our framework of orthodoxy. But one thing she's thought a lot about is her story, which is a pretty dark one. Raised by a mother she came to detest. Consumed by a bitterness that led to abusive uses of people and drugs and alcohol. Despair that she masked with cynicism. Yet all that led mysteriously to an encounter with the living God who claimed her and set her on a new and different path, one that has taken her far away from her old life, and yet one that still might raise questions for you and me. But that's not the point, is it? It's not for us to worry about her story. We've got our own story to worry about. We have our own journey to take from the empty tomb. And as sister Lamott writes, "I do not at all understand the mystery of grace—only that it meets us where we are but does not leave us where it found us."

The mystery of grace—that meets us where we are, but does not leave us where it found us.

"Do you love me?" The question is asked by the one who meets us where we are—perhaps with every hope to go back to the way life used to be, with every temptation to whittle down the resurrected life into something quaint and manageable. "Do you love me?" he asks, over and over.

"Yes, Lord, you know I love you."

And with grace he won't leave it at that. "Tend my sheep," he says.

For this grace meets us where we are, but does not leave us where it found us.

CHAPTER 15

Belongings

Psalm 46; Matthew 6:25–34

Several years ago my family and I were visiting that great entertainment center of the universe: Disney World. The Magic Kingdom. Now there is lots to do in Disney World, but I am pretty much the only roller-coaster rider in the family, which means I am often off by myself looking for the next thrill ride. It also meant, back before FastPass, a lot of waiting in long lines by myself. In one of these solo adventures I decided to take my turn on Space Mountain—the great roller coaster in the dark. As I approached the massive ride in front of me, I saw a father and his young son. The boy had barely met the height requirement to get into the ride, and that alone was reason enough, you could tell, for him to feel not only very proud but also very confident that Space Mountain was no big deal.

As I said, the lines for rides like Space Mountain are kind of long, and this one was particularly so. It wound throughout the building, and you'd find yourself walking through corridors of space paraphernalia and sounds that made it appear as if you were on your final walk to get into the Space Shuttle for liftoff. I noticed ahead of me that this little boy, who just moments before had been filled with a good share of bravado, all of a sudden wasn't feeling so courageous. He grew more and more silent and then began asking his father questions that betrayed a growing sense of reluctance. "How fast is the ride, Dad? Are there really big drops? Do you wear a seat belt? What happens if the seat belt doesn't work?" The father did his best to dispel the boy's fears, but his steps grew more and more timid. The expression on his face revealed a doubt that wondered if he was going to get off this ride alive.

Then came the moment of truth. Onto the platform the boy and his father were invited, with the next step being into the car that had yet to arrive. The boy froze. Panic filled his face, tears filled his eyes, and a tremble came to his lip. He so wanted to be brave. He so wanted to not let down his father, but there was no way he was getting into that car. The father then leaned over and whispered something into the boy's ear, something I could not hear. The little boy nodded his head, and with the last ounce of courage he could muster they took their place in the line for the next car. Moments later it arrived; they stepped in, sat down, and the mechanical harness pressed them into place. The boy stared straight ahead into the impending abyss, and the father stared straight at the boy. Off they went.

I'll never forget that scene as long as I live. Something about it spoke to so many things that go into the development of a human being—a child becoming an adult. You can unpack it and find a thousand lessons. In the end, though, there they were: parent and child. Child and parent. One of them not knowing what in heaven's name was going to happen, and the other knowing that everything—despite the darkness, despite the sudden drops, despite the invisible turns—in the end was going to be all right. They were going to get through the ride together.

It's been that way since the very beginning—facing into the fear of the unknown.

We don't know what goes through the mind of a child when he or she comes into the world. Consciousness is not very well formed in those early days of life. But it is safe to say that when we are babies we have no idea what is happening or what is going to happen to us. All we know is that we are cold and hungry, and the only way those things are going to be addressed is through an unmistakable wail. And if we are fortunate, a loving parent is close by whose instinct is to respond to our cry and give us what we need. In the best of families this relationship of trust and bond continues until those wonderful adolescent years, when children, despite what track record their parents have amassed, all of a sudden see their parents as the least intelligent and least trustworthy creatures on the planet.

But something about that picture of father and son heading into the darkness . . . that I think Jesus had this in mind when, in his teaching about the meaning and purpose of life, he continually referred to the God of heaven as Father. "Your Father in heaven," he would always say. It's how he spoke of his own Trinitarian relationship—Father, *Abba*, Daddy. There was something about this trust and bond between Creator and creature that Jesus was trying to point out to us. God has a yearning for us to see him as the Father—the trustworthy father who is taking his seat in the car as we make our way into the unknown darkness that is the future.

Certainly Jesus doesn't want us hung up on God's gender identity. God has no gender. This would be a far too limited view of God. Furthermore, for those who have had problematic or nonexistent relationships with fathers or mothers, this idea of God as a parent may be too high a hurdle. But at its very core it seems that what Jesus would want to point us to is the trust and the bond—the belief in the God of heaven who unmistakably attaches God's very self to us. We are on this ride together.

Inside the Presbyterian Church's *Book of Confession* there is a sixteenth-century confession written by our European reformer forbears that takes the form of a catechism, the Heidelberg Catechism: questions and answers of the faith. And when they put the catechism together I am sure they wrestled with what the first question should be. What question is of most importance to the being of God and to the human condition? They came up with Question #1: "What is your only comfort in life and in death?" The answer: "That I belong—body and soul, in life and in death—not to myself, but to my faithful Savior, Jesus Christ."

That I belong! Isn't that what we mean when we say, "I believe in God the Father Almighty"—that we belong to someone outside of ourselves? That we are not in this thing alone? Despite the great anxiety of life that says that we somehow have to face this thing called life on our own—that we have to go into the darkness by ourselves, that the world is just a bunch of chance accidents and it's only you and the dice—in the face of all that, the child of God stands forth and says, "I believe in God, the Father Almighty." I believe that God in his Almightiness attaches himself to me. I don't have to go through this life thinking that my only sense of belonging is to myself—but that I belong to God. That God will never let me go.

This is the Almightiness of God. Not that God somehow orchestrates every moment of my life and every action taking place around me. Not that somehow God is responsible for all the hurts and the hills and the hurdles of life; we tend to create a lot of those for ourselves. No, God in his Almightiness, in his Fatherly Almightiness, says to us that no matter what the darkness may hold, no matter how sudden the drop, no matter how unexpected the turn, nothing can pull me away from you.

Some of you have seen, I'm sure, the illustration that shows a dragon propped up against a tree. He is savoring his most recent meal. A medieval castle is in the distant background. The dragon is using a knight's lance as an after-dinner toothpick. Scattered all around are pieces of the knight's armor—breastplate, helmet, shield, and all the rest. Beneath the scene there is the caption:

> No matter how hard you work,
> No matter how right you are,
> Sometimes the dragon still wins.

It's a truth about life that we've all encountered in some way or another. Life ain't fair. Bad things happen to good people. Awful things occur to children who don't deserve them. The dragon wins sometimes. God's Almightiness is not about that. God's Almightiness is about the love he brings to it, the love that intercedes, the love that bears the same unfairness. That when the religious rulers mocked Jesus on the cross and implored him to come down and save himself, in his Almightiness God stayed on the cross to save the world. God's love promises that though the earth should change, though the mountains shake in the heart of the sea, though its waters roar and foam, we shall not fear—for the Lord of hosts is with us, the God of Jacob is our refuge.

The apostle Paul put it another way. "I am convinced," he said, "I am convinced . . . I am sure . . . I believe . . . that neither death nor life, nor angels, nor rulers, nor things present, nor things to come, nor powers, nor height, nor depth, nor anything else in all creation will be able to separate us from the love of God in Christ Jesus our Lord."

This is the Almightiness of God.

It makes me think of that time when I was in junior high and my parents took me on a trip behind what was then the Iron Curtain. One of our stops was Moscow, and while we were there my father was able to get two tickets for us to see the Soviets play Ireland in soccer. What a thrill for a ninth-grade boy. It was at Moscow's big soccer stadium, but we had no idea how to get there. We had someone write out the name of the stadium and the name of the hotel in Russian so that we could give it to the taxi driver in both directions. The first driver got us to the stadium, and we saw the Soviets beat the Irish team 1-0.

When the game was over we came out of the stadium—all sixty thousand of us—and found that there were no taxis. They had stopped running for the day. The only way to travel was by subway. The Moscow subway is beautiful, but it had only one station for this stadium of sixty thousand people. We walked with probably thirty thousand Russians—those who didn't have a car—to the one subway station, and my father could see that this was not going to be good. As we approached the station we found rows of Soviet soldiers forming a human funnel for us to squeeze into as we approached the one entrance. Thirty thousand people funneled into one entrance. This was one of those crowds where people get separated and crushed, and before we knew it we were inside the vortex.

As we started into it, my father turned around to me and saw panic on my face. He said, "I want you to do one thing and one thing only—I want you to grab onto the back of my belt. Grab on and don't even think about letting go. If you hold onto this belt then you will be all right." So in the darkness of the crushing crowd I held onto the back of the belt of this man in whose eye I had once been a gleam. And as the crush came, I held on. And I *held on*. I belonged. In the end I was all right. Tears streaming down my cheeks, ribs and arms a little bruised, but I was all right. Father got me through. Good news for an adolescent boy.

But you know what the better news is: this Father Almighty of whom we speak each Sunday—this Father Almighty in whom we believe—it's not about our grasp of him. It's about his grasp of us. Though the earth should change, though we don't know what tomorrow will bring, though life hurtles us into the darkness, though rulers and powers may wish to separate us, though the dragon sometimes wins, the good news is that we belong not to ourselves but to our faithful savior, Jesus Christ.

CHAPTER 16

Handmade

—∾—

Genesis 1:1–5; John 1:1–5; Revelation 21:1–5

I'VE BEEN THROUGH MANY PHASES in my life, as have we all. One of my phases was a bread-making phase. I had the idea in my head that one of the nicest gifts to give a person is a freshly baked loaf of bread. I had remembered the times when I had received such a gift myself—a cloth-covered, still-warm-from-the-oven loaf of bread, that when you cut it, steam rose with that fresh-baked dough scent awaiting a slice of butter that would melt even before you could get it to your mouth. Do you know what I am talking about? If so, I've probably lost you completely to your appetites.

So I decided to teach myself how to make bread. I got out an old Betty Crocker cookbook, found a whole-grain bread recipe, and went to work. I measured and I yeasted and I kneaded and I waited patiently for the dough to rise. When that first loaf came out of the oven I was so proud and so happy. I took it to the home of some friends, and the great joy of seeing the smiles on their faces when they opened the bag and turned back the cloth and smelled the fresh bread smell was even better than I thought it would be. There is nothing better than giving away some handmade, homemade gift—a gift of time and thought and care.

Though I had tried a loaf or two myself, as did my family, I was somewhat blind and senseless to the fact—and my family was too kind to tell me—that my loaves of bread were really not that good. Truth is, they were hard as rocks. Dental work was being damaged on these things, but I wasn't allowing myself to believe that. So I was prancing around the town and the congregation dispensing these freshly baked loaves of bread that, little did I know, people were using as doorstops. Reality finally came crashing down on me when I had delivered one of these fresh-baked gems to an older couple in the church, and about a week later they pulled up to our house. Out of the car they came with a nicely wrapped gift. *How nice*, I thought, *a little thank-you*. So I opened it . . . and it was a bread-making machine. I took the not-so-subtle hint and realized that breadmaking was probably not one of my spiritual gifts.

I will not forget, however, how those early bread days felt: the time, the energy, and the care that went into this creation that I would give as an offering, and the joy of seeing those smiles and hearing those "aaahs" when the cloth was pulled back and the fragrance filled the room. Something stirs deep within one's soul when you participate in the creative moment. We literally put ourselves into our creation.

Recall the story of the parents standing outside the nursery school waiting to pick up their children on the last school day before Christmas. When the time came, the door flew open and the children came running to their parents to give them the little Christmas gift they had been working on. One boy who was running, trying to put on his coat, and hold his gift all at the same time suddenly tripped, and the gift flew from his hands and landed on the floor with an obvious ceramic crash. At first the boy looked at the scattered pieces in stunned silence—and then he let forth an inconsolable wail. The father ran to him and, thinking to help, said, "That's all right, Son. It doesn't matter. It doesn't matter." But the mother, much wiser, said, "Oh, but it does matter . . . it does matter. It matters a great deal." And she leaned down and wept with her son.

Something is etched into our DNA, isn't there, when it comes to the creative process. It matters—our creativity. We are perhaps most in touch with ourselves when we are in touch with the creative side of our souls. It is one of the deep joys of life when we give and when we receive the fruits of creation. I suspect our congregation represents hundreds of refrigerators upon which are hanging the priceless treasures of our children and grandchildren. Refrigerator art, we call it. Every child produces it, and any decent parent or grandparent treasures these pieces of creativity, far more valuable than anything you would see hanging in the Metropolitan Museum of Art. And why make such a big deal? Because we know that this creative spark that lies deep within us matters a great deal. God forbid that we would ever dampen it.

Isn't it why we say, "I believe in God the Father Almighty, maker of heaven and earth"? Maker. Creator. We are pointing to something we believe to be so profoundly true—that this existence of ours is a creative existence. That it began with a creator and continues with a creator. The universe is a created and creating universe. God is a maker. It is who God is. "I believe in God the Father Almighty, *maker* of heaven and earth." We don't say, "Who once made heaven and earth." He is still in the business of making. We are not just offering some philosophical claim that God was there at the beginning—that he was merely the one who lit the fuse for the big bang and then sat down and watched *Wheel of Fortune*. You can't *stop* God from making and creating. Yes, he rested on that seventh day—but on that eighth day you can imagine that he was up at six and thinking about what's next.

God isn't done creating, you see. If we have the faith to call him "maker" in the creed, how foolish of us to think that all of sudden he ran out of good ideas when the sun went down on the sixth day. Annie Dillard, in *Pilgrim at Tinker Creek*, reminds us that of all the known forms of life that have ever existed, scientists guess that only about 10 percent are still living today. As full as the world seems to be right now, what we have is only a fraction of what God has been up to. Dillard writes,

> Multiplying ten times the number of living forms today yields a profusion that is quite beyond what I consider thinkable. Why so many forms? Why not just that [first] hydrogen atom? [No], the creator goes off on one wild, specific tangent after another, or millions

> simultaneously, with an exuberance that would seem to be unwarranted, and with an abandoned energy sprung from an unfathomable font. What is going on here? The point of the dragonfly's terrible lip, the giant water bug, birdsong, or the beautiful dazzle and flash of sunlighted minnows, is not that it all fits together like clockwork . . . , but that it all flows so freely wild, like the creek, that it all surges in such a free, fringed tangle. . . . The creator loves pizzazz.

So when we say that we believe in the maker, aren't we saying that at the very beginning and at the very center of existence there is this creative force, this three-person artist, this atomic explosion of paint and clay that wishes to envelop us and make us into creators ourselves? Henri Bergson, the French Nobel Prize–winning philosopher, said that, "In creation God undertook to create creators." This is the image of God implanted within us. This is where we find our deepest joy—when we are about the act of creating. We are most in touch with the Creator when we join him in his creating. This is when the soul most stirs.

Donald Frey was an engineer back in the early 1960s. He worked for the Ford Motor Company designing new car models. It was a good living. He was ensconced in the day-to-day trip back and forth to the office using his slide rule and pumping out cars like the Edsel and the Ford Falcon. Then came the moment of truth, when one night at dinner with his family, his kids turned to him and said, "Dad, your cars stink." What do you mean? he asked. "I don't know," they said. "There's just no pizzazz."

Donald Frey, who died just a few years ago, was fond of telling people that that was the first day of the creation of the Ford Mustang—one of the great innovations in automotive history, what we call today "a classic." "There's just no pizzazz," they said.

Do you see what we get invited into when we say that God is maker? We get invited into the pizzazz! We get invited into the creative spirit of God, who is still up to something. Like that taxi driver who picked up a guy from National Airport in Washington, DC—a tourist from overseas who just wanted to be driven to see the sites. So they traveled around and saw all the monuments, museums, and government buildings, and then the cabbie took him past the National Archives. When they drove by, the tourist could see the great etched phrase on the front of the building: "The Past Is Prologue." The tourist, not knowing English very well, asked what it meant. The driver said, "It means—you ain't seen nothin' yet!"

Behold, God says, I make all things new. I'm looking for some pizzazz. Not just from within Godself—but from us! The created creators. This is the love language of God—that God doesn't just create unresponsive lumps of clay. But God forms us from the dust of earth and breathes life into us, makes us come alive, and animates us. This is God's great joy. But an even greater joy of God's is when the animated ones—the created ones—start creating on their own, taking the substance of the universe and making something.

Consider the great statements of scripture when God invokes the word, "make." "I will make of you a great nation," he says to Abraham. "I will make with you a new covenant," he says to Jeremiah. "Go and make disciples of all nations," he tells the disciples. "I am making all things new," he tells the church.

Think of Jesus' great story about the three servants who are responsible for different shares of talents while the master is gone. The five-talent servant invests the five talents and makes five talents more. The two-talent servant invests the two talents and makes two talents more. The one-talent servant just lets his one talent sit there. Buries it even. Hides it. Protects it. And the master comes back and says, What did you do with the talent? That's the maker's question, too. What did you do with the stuff I gave you? And the servant says, You know, I was afraid. I held back. I had the lump of clay but I didn't put my fingers into it. I had my canvas, but I left it blank. I had my 401(k), but I kept it safe for a rainy day. I had twenty-four hours a day, but I spent a lot of it in front of the TV, on the golf course, and out to lunch. I had so much, but I didn't breathe life into it. I didn't invest. I didn't take the risk. I didn't make anything.

The master responds, "Didn't you know that I am the maker? Didn't you know that I love pizzazz? Didn't you know that I breathed life into you? Didn't you know that letting it sit there wasn't one of the options? Didn't you know that the great joy of life comes when you are taking what I've given you and you are making something of it—something that speaks love, something that reveals beauty, something that shows the world you care, something that points to the maker of heaven and earth? It doesn't matter that your bread might taste like a rock. The point is that you tried."

Only you and God know what your talent account is. Only you and God know what is possible for you to do tomorrow, next week, or this coming year. Only you and God know what you could do to make a difference. Only you and God know what gifts you have to share, what time you have to offer, what skills you can employ, what money you can give. Only you and God know that. God knows there is beauty still to be shared. God knows there are poor people still to be fed. God knows there is a creation to be nurtured. God knows there is peace to be made. God knows there are little minds that need shaping. God knows. The maker knows. It's why he is still making. And what the maker also knows is the joy to be found when we make some pizzazz with him.

CHAPTER 17

Signs of the Times

—∿∿—

Isaiah 7:10–16; Matthew 1:18–25

When I was a senior in college I was struggling with what to do with my life. I had pretty much spent my teenage years lauding the fact that I was not going into the family business. Everybody in my family was a pastor, and I was bound and determined to show them I was my own man. So political science was the major I picked, with every intention of pursuing government service of some kind. It was the way I thought I could best serve God. But the hound of heaven had other ideas in mind, and as I entered my senior year, an interest in the church began to grow in me. I fought it, of course, at every turn; the stubborn pride of a young man in his early twenties trying to differentiate himself from the family is a powerful force. Nevertheless I felt at home in the church, and a voice in the back of my mind grew louder and louder: *Steve, you belong in the church.*

At about that time the political organization at my college of which I served as chairperson was hosting a US senator,

Mark Hatfield from Oregon, to speak to the college community. It was a big deal for me to host Senator Hatfield, as he had been a political hero of mine for quite some time. Before his speech I was even given a few minutes alone with him to talk. He was very interested in what we were doing there on campus and curious about what I was considering doing after college. (I had this hidden hope that he might offer me a job.) But then I made a mistake. I told him that I was struggling with my call to service, and I wasn't sure whether God was calling me to serve the government or the church. Then the senator said to me, "I know you're not asking my advice, but if I were you I would test first the call to the church. Government will always be there. But test first the call to the church." Well, there went my job offer! But those words bore into the center of my soul. I don't know why, but that conversation for me became fateful. A tipping point. I took those words to heart, testing first the call to the church, and I've never looked back.

Senator Hatfield never learned how important those words were. He never could have imagined that night that a third of a century later the young man would look back and count those words pregnant with future meaning.

In the prophecy related in Isaiah 7:10–16, Isaiah is before Ahaz, the king of Israel, and Israel is being threatened. The prophet challenges the king to ask for a sign from God. But the king refuses. He says it's not right to challenge God to present a sign. So the prophet speaks for God and says, "OK, even though you won't ask for a sign, God is going to give you one anyway. Look, the young woman is with child and shall bear a son and shall name him Immanuel." The prophet, as he does throughout, speaks to his times. The king is to look for a sign in those days—and the sign is to be a young woman with child, bearing a son and naming him Immanuel. We don't know who this ended up to be in the times of Ahaz, but that was the sign he was to look for. But who was to know in those days that Isaiah's sixth-century BC words were pregnant (excuse the term) with future meaning? Six centuries later a virgin is with child and bears a son and names him Emmanuel—which means God with us. Matthew the Gospel writer looks back and remembers that fateful conversation between prophet and king and hears words pregnant with future meaning—and sees them in the story of Bethlehem. The sign of those times was to be the sign for these times.

More than 150 years ago an embattled president takes a half-day train ride to a backwoods town in central Pennsylvania that fatefully had hosted three days of brutal war, leaving scores of thousands wounded and killed. He was to dedicate a cemetery. That was all. He was to follow in the program a silver-tongued orator of the times whose speech would last two hours! Two hours . . . and 13,607 words! (My congregants shouldn't feel so bad about my sermons.) The beleaguered president, after applauding, stands at the podium and, with no benefit of a microphone, reads his speech of 270 words. "Four score and seven years ago . . ." How was he to know what those words might really mean? How was he to know that they would be etched in marble and in the minds of millions of American schoolchildren? They pointed to the signs of those times and the signs of our times.

The Advent characters were most certainly sign pointers and sign watchers. Zechariah takes his turn to offer the sacrifice in the temple, and the message comes that his barren Elizabeth will bear a child. How can this be? He is also given a sign: his speech will be taken from him. And now he knows.

A young virgin, Mary, receives an unexpected visit from an angel named Gabriel. The angel tells her that she will conceive in her womb and bear a son and name him Jesus. And Mary asks the obvious question: How can this be since I have no husband? The angel says, Look for the sign—your cousin Elizabeth in her old age has also conceived. The one who was called barren is six months along.

Joseph gets the word that his teenage betrothed is with child through no help from him. He decides to quietly and gentlemanly divorce her—but then comes a dream and an angel and the words: Be not afraid. He sees in them a sign that somehow he is to stick around and take Mary as his wife and name the child to be Emmanuel.

The angels sing glory to God in the highest and point the shepherds to nearby Bethlehem to find the child born to them—the savior who is Christ the Lord. "And this will be a sign for you—you will find a babe wrapped in swaddling cloths and lying in a manger." A manger? Yes, a manger. Because it is a sign.

Wise men from the east notice an unusual star in the night sky, and they are not sure what to make of it except that it must be some celestial sign. They trust their gut to follow it, because that is what you do with signs. You follow them.

That is, of course, if you see them. And that may be the question: Do we see them?

The Advent characters looked for the signs. Strange visitors became angels. Unusual anatomical happenings became the power of the Most High. Messages left in dreams became the word of God. Quirky heavenly movements became stars to follow. Do you see what I'm saying? If anything can be said about the Advent characters, they left room in their world for God to say something, for God to do something, for God to show a sign. We too eagerly leave ourselves off the hook when we read the Advent story and say, "Lucky them, they got real signs! Angels and unexpected pregnancies and dreams and falling stars! We want God to do the same thing again." But God doesn't do the same thing again. God never does the same thing again. Behold, God says and is always saying, I am doing a new thing.

Is it possible that God is filling the world with new signs—that the multitude of the heavenly host is filling the heavens and the earth—that signs are appearing before our very eyes but we don't see them? So busy are we looking for the old signs that we don't see the new signs? That the modern world, so enamored with human ingenuity, has become so small that God has no room to move, to act, to speak? We seem to have a small answer for just about everything that we forget that maybe God has some big things to say to us. Lord knows that Joseph could have chalked up that strange dream of a talking angel to the onions he ate the night before, but he didn't. The world was bigger than that; it had room for God to speak, to move, to act.

Is your world big enough for God to speak, move, and act? Are you leaving yourself open to the possibility that signs might be about, maybe even in the simplest of things? That God is trying to say something—if only to announce that he is Emmanuel—God with us . . . in the now, in the present, in the times?

Annie Dillard, in her great book *Pilgrim at Tinker Creek*, muses for us about the time she spent at a simple creek outside of Roanoke, Virginia. All she did in her strolls to and beside the creek is watch and look for the signs, to watch inside a world that was big enough for God to speak. At one point she pauses before one section of the brook and writes,

> It is sheer coincidence that my hunk of the creek is strewn with boulders. I never merited this grace, that when I face upstream I scent the virgin breath of mountains, I feel a spray of mist on my cheeks and lips, I hear a ceaseless splash and susurrus, a sound of water not merely poured smoothly down air to fill a steady pool, but tumbling live about, over, under, around, between, through an intricate speckling of rock. It is sheer coincidence that upstream from me the creek's bed is ridged in horizontal croppings of sandstone. I never merited this grace, that when I face upstream I see the light on the water careening towards me, inevitably, freely, down a graded series of terraces like the balanced winged platforms on an infinite, inexhaustible

> font. "Ho [she quotes from Isaiah], if you are thirsty, come down to the water; ho, if you are hungry, come and sit and eat." This is the present, at last . . . This is the now, this flickering, broken light, this air that the wind of the future presses down my throat, pumping me buoyant and giddy with praise.
>
> My God, I look at the creek. It is the answer to Merton's prayer, "Give us time!"

Talk about a world big enough for God to speak, to act, to move, and to beckon us into the divine presence. Emmanuel . . . God with us. For this is what happens to the characters of Christmas—because the world is filled with the possibility that God might be up to something—when they see the sign and hear the sign. They consider the possibility that God might be wanting them for something. God is up to something, and he has me in mind for a part.

Might that be true for you? That God is up to something, and he has you in mind for a part? A story that includes a teenage virgin and a senior citizen bearing a child would suggest to us that no one reading this is exempt from playing a part, if only we would see the signs. Are you seeing the signs? Is the world big enough for God to show up and, despite your circumstance, still say something?

Years ago *LIFE* magazine did a little spread where they asked a bunch of different people to write about the meaning of life. They asked celebrities, authors, and statesmen to reflect on this question. They also asked an eleven-year-old boy named

Jason Gaes, a cancer victim, about the meaning of life, and this is what he had to say:

> Why are we born was a really hard paper to write. I think God made us each born for a different reason. If God gives you a great voice maybe he wants you to sing. Or else if God makes you 7 feet tall maybe he wants you to play for the Lakers or the Celtics. When my friend Kim died from her cansur I asked my Mom if god was going to make Kim die when she was only 6 why did he make her born at all. But my Mom said even thogh she was only 6 she changed people's lifes. What that means is like her brother or sister could be the siontist that discovers the cure for cansur and they decided to do that because of Kim. And like me too. I used to wonder why did God pick on me and give me cansur. Maybe it was because he wanted me to be a dr. who takes care of kids with cansur so when they say, "Dr. Jason, I get so scared" or "you don't know how weird it is to be the only bald kid in your whole school." And I can say, "Oh yes I do. I had cansur and look at all my hair now."

Signs of the times, we might say—in a world big enough for God to speak, to act, to move, and to invite us in some small way to take our part in the divine presence.

CHAPTER 18

Nevertheless

—∿∿—

Isaiah 35:1–10

You may recall the story of the little boy who was racing around the house while his mother was getting ready for dinner guests. He was making a mess here and making a mess there. His mom was always having to stop what she was doing to clean up something he had done, and she was just about at her limit. It was then that the little boy on his way out of the house ran past the beautifully set dining room table, and his belt buckle caught hold of the lace tablecloth, pulling it and everything on it off the table with an unceremonious crash. The mother lost it. She chased her son out the door and watched him climb underneath the porch. She was just about ready to go in after him, but she realized that the guests would be coming soon so she decided to leave it for her husband to handle. When her husband came home, the mom told him of all the boy did that day and how the icing on the cake was the yanking of the tablecloth and that he better go out there and have a talk with his son.

The father went out and got down on his hands and knees and starting crawling under the porch. Way in the back he saw two little eyes staring at him. So he kept crawling toward his son, and then he heard his little boy say, "Is she after you, too?"

That story brings to mind my own little "Is she after you, too?" story. It happened at Christmastime. I was around ten or eleven years old, and I had noticed underneath our Christmas tree a five-pound bag of birdseed that someone had given to my father as a white-elephant gift. Well, we didn't have a bird, but my best buddy, Richard Norris, did. So I picked up that bag of birdseed and found my mother and asked her if I could take the birdseed over to my buddy Richard's so that they could use it for their bird. She said I could. Now, my mother had just finished cleaning the house for the imminent arrival of my grandparents. So excited that I could take this birdseed to my friend's, I began to swing the bag around and around. I was standing in the hall next to about five different rooms. Well, you know what happened. The bag broke, and I became a human birdseed spreader. I did this right in front of my mother, who had just finished cleaning the house, who was expecting the visit of family, and who took great pride in a spotless home. I'd never before seen the look on her face I saw then. I had never before heard that tone in her voice. My life began to flash in front of my eyes. She pointed me to the vacuum cleaner and told me that if every last piece of birdseed was not picked up from the five rooms into which I had spread it, I might wish for the wrath of God over the wrath that was in store for me from her.

I can only imagine that in the craziness of Christmastime, such a scene is not necessarily a rarity. Just make your way to a crowded shopping mall, airport, or restaurant, and you will likely find some frayed nerves and some stressed pilgrims—and it doesn't take much for tempers to flare and emotions to show.

For me—the human birdseed spreader—I am blessed to be able to say that the emotion and anger I was experiencing from my mother were exceptions—an aberration, something I had never seen. And so it didn't surprise me a few minutes later as I was Electroluxing every nook and cranny in every room, seeking to skirt the imminent doom that was promised, when my mother came back and saw the tears in my eyes and said, "It's all right. You know I love you. It's just that I had worked so hard." And she got down on her knees and we picked up birdseed together.

I was fortunate to live in what I would call a "nevertheless" home. A nevertheless home is a home where as a child you can mess up, you can disappoint, you can fail to meet expectations, you can spread birdseed throughout the house—you can be a kid and do stupid, kidlike things—and *nevertheless* you were still going to be loved. You were still going to be cherished. You were still going to be prized as the greatest. A family of four boys can drive a mom and a dad crazy, and yet nevertheless we knew that we could do nothing that would ever cause them to withdraw their love. I understand that not every home is that way. Some of you grew up in homes where the love was conditional, where tempers were not the exception, where value was tied to performance, or where abuse was the primary language. In many homes there is not a *nevertheless.*

In light of this, perhaps it is good for us to be in the thirty-fifth chapter of the book of Isaiah. Isaiah is the oracle of the prophet who is speaking to Israel in and around the heartbreaking time of the siege and sacking of Jerusalem at the hands of the Babylonians. And for the first thirty-three or thirty-four chapters—a part of what many call First Isaiah—the message that ushers forth from the prophet is a message of warning and doom. Isaiah warns the people that the wrath of God is imminent. Israel has displeased the Lord, and the result will be the destruction of their homeland. They will be dragged from their homes. They will be displaced for generations. This first section of Isaiah doesn't have a lot of good news. Israel has displeased and disappointed. They have not measured up to expectations. Bad things are soon to happen. And sure enough, Israel is sacked and the people are dragged from their homes and the promised land seems to hold no promise anymore.

But then comes chapter 35—and a new voice. In chapter 35 a new movement begins . . . and a new message is proclaimed. Yes, Israel, you have displeased, you have disappointed, and you are paying for your sins. Yes, Israel, the very worst has happened: God has allowed you to pay the price for your folly. Yet, nevertheless . . . the day is coming when wilderness and the dry land shall be glad, the desert shall rejoice and blossom. The day will come when they shall see the glory of the Lord and the majesty of our God. The ransomed of the Lord shall return and come to Zion with singing; everlasting joy shall be upon their heads; they shall obtain joy and gladness, and sorrow and sighing shall flee away. God is not giving up, Israel. God is not holding your sins against you. God is not abandoning you to endless captivity. All of a sudden, Israel hears that their God is a nevertheless God. You have disappointed. You have displeased. You have been very foolish. Yet nevertheless, God will not withhold his love. Nevertheless, God will not forget you. Nevertheless, God will deliver you from your own folly.

The joy of which the prophet speaks is a joy that comes from knowing that God is a nevertheless God. Joy comes in knowing that, though we do enough to mess things up, mess ourselves up, mess the world up, God's ultimate word to us is *nevertheless*. Nevertheless I will still love you. Nevertheless I will still save you. Nevertheless I will still forgive you. We can do nothing to keep God from saying "nevertheless."

Remember that scene in Charles Dickens's *A Christmas Carol* when the Spirit of Christmas Present takes Ebenezer Scrooge to the home of his nephew, who is with his friends and family enjoying the Christmas feast? Everybody in the room—not aware that Scrooge is listening and watching—gets to talking about crotchety old Scrooge—laughing at his miserly, humbug ways—and how the pathetic old man can't seem to find any ounce of mirth for the holiday. But the nephew won't join in, the nephew who makes it his practice every year to stop by and wish the old humbug a Merry Christmas and invite him to their home for the feast. The nephew sees the old uncle as something different than do the rest of the assembled. He won't give in to their mockery. He realizes that the man is paying for his own folly. Finally he raises his glass and offers a toast: "A Merry Christmas and a Happy New Year to the old man, whatever he is," he says. "He wouldn't take it from me, but may he have it nevertheless."

May he have it nevertheless. And to hear the voice of the nephew is for Scrooge his Isaiah 35, the joy of discovering that despite himself, he is loved . . . nevertheless.

A lot is said about how you are supposed to feel at Christmastime. There's a lot of talk about holly and jolly and merry and happy and peace and goodwill—and all of it is what we would hope not just for ourselves but for all whom we love. But holly and jolly and merry and happy seem so much to be tied to the circumstances of our lives. The shifting fortunes of life can make us either very, very happy—or very, very sad. Hard to wish a holly, jolly Christmas to someone who's just lost a spouse, a job, or one's health. And that's why it is so important for us to hear the greeting of the prophet who wishes us something different. He wishes us joy, and joy is not holly or happy or merry. Joy is something else. Joy is when you come to know of God's nevertheless. Joy is when you come to know that you are the child of a God who will never stop saying "nevertheless" to you. Although life and folly may have led you to the wrong places, although circumstances may have your mind and heart in the shadows, joy is when you know that, despite it all, God's word to you is "nevertheless." Nevertheless, you are loved. Nevertheless, salvation will come. Nevertheless, the glory of the Lord will someday be revealed.

Might we call it the mistletoe that the angels hang over the weary old world? Despite the craziness we tend to inflict upon ourselves and others, God hangs this mistletoe over creation and says, "Nevertheless, unto you is born this day in the city of David, a Savior who is Christ the Lord."

Richard Selzer, a plastic surgeon, tells the story of a patient whose surgery under his hand did not go as planned—the result being a nerve in her face mistakenly severed and her mouth unable to straighten. Selzer recounts the moment at her bedside along with her husband when he delivers the bad news.

The young woman speaks. "Will my mouth always be like this?"

"Yes," he says, "it will. It is because the nerve was cut."

She nods and is silent. But then the young man, the husband, smiles.

"I like it," he says. "It's kind of cute."

And then Dr. Selzer notices the man bending to kiss her crooked mouth. And as he does he can see the young man bend his lips to accommodate hers—just to show that their kiss still works.

Nevertheless.

It's where the joy is, isn't it? It's under the mistletoe. The word comes from the heavens that despite all that has gone on, all we have done to tax the patience of the creator God, and how far we've flung the seed, the word still hangs over us—*nevertheless*—just to show us that our kiss still works.

CHAPTER 19

The Things We Don't Have to Do

Matthew 5:38–48; Luke 3:10–14

LAST CHRISTMAS EVE DURING THE day, a few hours before the Christmas Eve services, there was a hospital call for me to make in a neighboring town. When I was through visiting and on my way home, I stopped by the local Starbucks drive-thru (something I seldom do) to pick up a cup of coffee. I waited in the car line and placed my order, but when I got to the window, the Starbucks lady told me that my drink was free.

"Free," I said. "How does that work?"

"Oh," she said, "the guy ahead of you bought it for you and said to say, 'Merry Christmas.'" We were pretty far from home, so I was almost certain that my treat came from a stranger, somebody unknown to me—a little treat I could never pay back. Clearly this stranger did not have to do anything. There would be no credit given, no thank-you note in the mail. Of course, we kept the string going, paying it forward, and the lady behind me got herself a little Christmas gift, too. Lord knows how long it continued. It was a nice moment.

A few minutes later I had one more stop to make on my way home, at a local drugstore. When I had made my purchases, I was back in my car exiting the parking lot, and two lines of cars were merging into the one parking lot exit. It was a busy shopping day, of course. Nevertheless, each driver was taking turns merging into the one line, with the exception of the woman in the other line across from me. The car ahead of her took its turn, so it was my turn to file in—but for whatever reason she was not going to let that happen. Hugging the bumper of the guy before her and without even giving me a glance, she jumped the line. *Interesting*, I thought. *She must be in quite a hurry on this busy shopping day.* Imagine my surprise when I finally got behind her and saw the sticker on her back bumper that said, "Jesus is the reason for the season."

The juxtaposed experiences, on Christmas Eve of all days, gave me some pause and obviously has stuck in my mind ever since. And I guess this stuck-in-my-mind part has me wondering about the impression you and I make in the things we choose to do and choose not to do. We have to do a lot of things in this world—pay taxes, be good to our children, cut the lawn, change the oil, take no more than ten things to the express checkout line in the supermarket. But what about the things we don't have to do—the things that nobody expects, the surprise gestures of grace, the unusual kindnesses that a calculated world has learned not to count on, the free coffee from the guy in front of you? If Jesus is the reason for the season, then what does that mean about the things we have to do and don't have to do?

Is this what Jesus was trying to say in the Sermon on the Mount, when he stated, "You know, you are the salt of the earth"? You are the ones who can bring flavor to the world. Whatever you do and however you do it, it really matters. When salt is in the mix, everybody notices it.

On a certain Thanksgiving when I was young, my mother had just returned home from having surgery and was recuperating. It was left to my father and me to cook Thanksgiving dinner for our family and some invited friends. This was, of course, the first mistake. My father doled out assignments, and I was given the task of making the mashed potatoes. Translated for me, that meant, Go out and buy a box of Hungry Jack's Instant mashed potatoes. So I did, and I duly followed the instructions on the back, whipped up a batch of something that looked like mashed potatoes, and placed it proudly on the table. Once grace was said, the first person who took a bite promptly spit it back onto his plate—as did the second person and the third person. This was not a good sign. I've since learned from the Food Channel that people spitting what you've cooked back onto their plates is not high praise. Turns out that in my careful study of the directions, what I thought said *tablespoon* of salt said *teaspoon* of salt. What a difference a tablespoon makes!

So Jesus said, You are the salt of the earth, and when salt is in the mix, everybody notices it. Whatever you do, and however you do it, it matters.

Not much further into the Sermon on the Mount, Jesus gets more specific: "If anyone strikes you on the right cheek, turn the other also; and if anyone wants to sue you and take your coat, give your cloak as well; and if anyone forces you to go one mile, go also the second mile. Give to everyone who begs from you, and do not refuse anyone who wants to borrow from you. And while you are busy loving the people who you know are going to love you back, go ahead and love the ones that hate you, too." All of a sudden Jesus is speaking of this very interesting life of doing the things that nobody expects you to do.

John the Baptist in Luke's Gospel speaks about the salty life when he says, "If you've got two coats, share with the one who has none. If you've got food in your cupboard after dinner, give it to the one whose closet is empty"—this interesting life of doing the things that nobody expects you to do.

It reminds me of a story of two farmers who were good friends. One went off for the weekend to a Christian conference, and when he came back, his friend asked him about the conference. The farmer said, "I learned a lot about the Christian life."

"Really," said his friend. "What did you learn?"

He said, "Well, it kind of goes like this. If you had two tractors and you knew I had none, would you give me one of your tractors?"

"Well, of course," his friend said. "If had two tractors I'd give you one."

The first farmer said, "And if you had two hay wagons and you knew I had none, would you give me one of your hay wagons?"

His friend said, "Well, yes, if I had two hay wagons I'd give you one."

"And if you had two cows and you knew I had none, would you give me one of your cows?"

"Doggone, Charlie, that's not fair. You know I have two cows!"

Life gets interesting when we do the things we don't have to do.

Almost sixty years ago, a little girl by the name of Joan Lancaster, who lived in Sarasota on Bayshore Road, finished reading a children's story written by a quite famous English author named, you guessed it, C. S. Lewis. It was 1954. By that time Lewis had already been on the cover of *Time* magazine, and his books had made him an international phenomenon. When the little girl finished reading one of these children's books—*The Lion, the Witch, and the Wardrobe*—she decided that she was going to write this author a letter and learn more about the stories. With all childlike innocence she wrote her note, put it in an envelope along with a drawing and picture of herself, and from her home she sent it off. Imagine her surprise when a couple of weeks later in her mailbox a letter had arrived from Mr. Lewis. Handwritten, five paragraphs long.

In part this is what Mr. Lewis wrote this elementary-school-age girl:

> Dear Joan Lancaster:
> Thank you very much for your kind letter with beautiful painting and interesting photo which reached me today.
>
> I am so glad you like the Narnian books, and it was nice of you to tell me. There are to be seven stories altogether. . . . The 7th is already written, but still only in pen-and-ink, and I have not quite decided yet what to call it. Sometimes I think of calling it *The Last King of Narnia*, and sometimes, *Night Falls on Narnia*. Which do you think sounds best?
>
> I was at a zoo last week and saw the real lions: also some perfectly lovely bears nursing their cubs.
>
> How lucky you are to have a pool.
>
> With love to your brother and yourself.
>
> Yours ever,
>
> C. S. Lewis

Imagine the thrill of that little Sarasota girl opening that mailbox and that envelope and reading those words. Wow! And, of course, no one would have faulted the famous author, speaker, and lecturer for not taking the time out of his busy schedule to write a note to a young fan a couple thousand miles away. Clearly not something he had to do. Amazing, though, what a little salt will do.

Enough so that Joan Lancaster wrote him another note with more pictures, asking more questions. And sure enough there came another response. And then she wrote another letter—to which came another response. This happened twenty-six times, until just a few weeks before the author died. Twenty-six times. The things you don't have to do! And little Joan Lancaster was just one of hundreds to whom Lewis wrote in the same way.

You are the salt of the earth. Whatever you do, and however you do it, can make a huge difference. Amazing what a tablespoon of salt will do.

When I was a little boy, the youngest of four sons, soon after one of my brothers received a diagnosis of severe mental handicaps, my mother employed a woman to be a mother's helper. Betty was a mother herself with nine children of her own, but to make ends meet she came into our home two days a week. She became in many ways a part of our family and made the four of us boys her boys, too. After years of this we moved away. And as these things go, we lost touch with Betty. Imagine my surprise when I got a call some forty years later from Betty's daughter saying that Betty was in her last few days, but she couldn't go without calling her McConnell boys. So Betty got on the phone and said, "Stevie, I just called to say I love you. And there hasn't been a day when I didn't pray for you." Oh my gosh—talk about the things you don't deserve.

The things we don't have to do.

Carl Rowan, the prize-winning columnist of a few decades ago, spoke often of the influence in his life of a woman named Bessie

Gwinn. Bessie instructed Rowan at Bernard High School while he was growing up in McMinnsville, teaching him Shakespeare and Chaucer and Milton and the scriptures. She also taught Carl about similes and metaphors and hyperbole. After graduating from high school and college, Carl went on to become an accomplished journalist, nominated one year for the Pulitzer Prize.

When Bessie turned eighty-five, she was to be honored at a testimonial dinner by a group of her students and fellow teachers, and Carl was invited to come and say a few words. As fate would have it, he had been invited on the same night to attend a White House dinner hosted by then-president Jimmy Carter. How often in a lifetime do you get invited to a White House dinner? Rowan sat down and wrote this letter in response to the president's invitation:

> Dear Mr. President: I received your letter three days after I had agreed to speak a few words at a dinner honoring the wonderful high school teacher who taught me to write. I know you will not miss me at your dinner but she might at hers.
>
> Sincerely yours,
> Carl Rowan

The things you don't have to do. The tablespoon of salt that will never be forgotten.

I know I may sound like a broken record when I say that you don't have to go far to be reminded that the world can be a pretty tough place. Bad things happen to good people, and good things happen to bad people. The rain falls on the just and the unjust. Everybody is on their guard, and everybody wants what's coming to them. And there always seems to be a fight over what we really have to do for each other. Who owes who what? The result is a dog-eat-dog world that can leave a lot of us rolling our eyes, smirking, and saying, "Whatever."

But then I walk into our church on a Tuesday afternoon and see tables and tables of adults side by side with kids who need a little help with their schoolwork—and I look at these volunteering adults and say, "You know, you don't have to do this." And then I poke my head into our food pantry and see volunteers graciously packing and handing out bags of food to people down on their luck, and I say, You don't have to do this. Then I stop over at the local elementary school and see volunteers taking classrooms of kids under their wings, and I say, You don't have to do this. I see ministry teams gathered for meetings, I see Sunday school teachers teaching, I see sweating people tending the grounds, I see strangers helping strangers to their cars, I see offering envelopes going into the plate from people who barely have enough to pay the rent, I see missionaries going to Central America, I see advisors hanging out with teenagers, I see and I see and I see . . . and I say, You don't have to do this.

And of course we don't. And of course we do.

For we are, Jesus says, the salt of the earth.

CHAPTER 20

Down Market

—᠁—

Jeremiah 32:1–15

SOMEWHERE ALONG THE WAY MOST of us have crossed paths with Cervantes's classic tale, *Don Quixote*—the story of the delusional man, Alonso Quijano, who had read far too many tales of chivalry and become convinced that this is the life to which he has been called himself. He turns himself into a knight, Don Quixote; dons a battered suit of armor; and recruits a local farmer, Sancho Panza, to be his squire. The two gallop the Spanish countryside in Don Quixote's chivalric pursuits. In windmills he sees giants, in holy men he sees captors, in taverns he sees castles, and in peasant girls he sees queens. More often than not, he views benign moments as crises and steps in where he is, in fact, not needed. He often makes matters worse with his hope of bringing justice to a cruel world. Published four hundred years ago and considered perhaps the first great modern novel, *Don Quixote* raises the age-old existential question about how to view our mission in the world. How do we face the realities that surround us? What are we to do with the events that unfold before us? Must we courageously engage with fantasies of making some kind of difference, sticking our nose into places where we may not be needed or welcomed? Or should we cynically stand back and pessimistically watch as the world seemingly goes to hell in a handbasket? Is it crazier to think that you can change the world for the better, or to think that if the world is going to change, it will change undoubtedly for the worse?

In the Broadway version of the story, *Man of La Mancha*, Don Quixote addresses the question this way: "Too much sanity may be madness. And maddest of all, to see life as it is and not as it should be."

And maddest of all, to see life as it is and not as it should be.

If you are wondering where in scripture you might look to find the maddest of all the biblical characters, you don't need to look much further than the section in the Hebrew scriptures called the Prophets. The prophets of the Old Testament are continually seeing the world very differently from most around them, always raising the contrary view. When Israel thinks it is making itself more secure, the prophets warn them of their insecurity. When Israel gets obsessed over its religious duties and its piety, the prophets shake a stick and say, Remember the orphans and widows. And when Israel and Jerusalem despair over their sacking and captivity, the prophets say, "Comfort, comfort my people. . . . Make straight in the desert a highway for our God. Every valley shall be lifted up and every mountain and hill be made low . . . for the glory of the Lord will be revealed."

The prophets, in other words, see things that most people cannot see. And what they see is that the God of Israel is somehow working his purposes out. They see that the God of Israel is a God of covenant, who makes and keeps his promises, who loves his people and will never let them go, who is not above or below the attempt to make his people into a holy and righteous people. They see a God who holds in one hand the scales of justice and in the other hand the mantle of grace. And the prophets don their armor and walk upon the plains of Palestine and give witness to the promises and purposes of God. In other words, they hold on to the view that as bad as the world might seem to be, somehow God will redeem all this. Somehow God will not renege on his promise. And in the face of certain scorn, ridicule, and derision, in the face of the great cynicism and skepticism of the day, the prophets see it as their mission to do something about it, to take on the side of the redemptive God who is working his purposes out.

Nowhere perhaps is this courageous calling more exemplified than in Jeremiah 32, in which the prophet is witnessing the destruction of Jerusalem—the walls tumbled, the city sacked, the people of God being carried off into captivity in Babylon, and the pundits all around saying that this is the end. So in the face of the world going to hell, the prophet decides that now is the time to buy some land. Now is the time to stake a claim. Now is the time to put his money where his mouth is and say, Someday we will return. Someday we will come back home. Someday the glory of the Lord will be revealed and all flesh will see it together, and there will be a real estate boom right here in Jerusalem. While caravans of people and possessions are leaving town, Jeremiah says not to forget the promises of God. Don't forget the faithfulness of God. Don't forget that God will not let his people go. Someday they are going to build on this land. Jeremiah held onto his hope, and he acted on it. Down payment on a field that wouldn't see a house for a hundred years. Crazy old Jeremiah waving a deed to a property that would lie empty for four generations. Getting laughed at, reviled, scorned, abused—all because he saw something that nobody else could see: the promises and purposes of a God who would stay true to the covenant.

"Blessed are you when people revile you and persecute you and utter all kinds of evil against you falsely on my account. Rejoice and be glad, for your reward is great in heaven, for in the same way they persecuted the prophets who were before you" (Matthew 5:11–12).

It is so easy for you and me to give in to the cynicism of the day, to look outside the walls of our houses and see the amassing armies of a changing world where things aren't the way they used to be, to read the headlines and worry that things are just getting worse and worse. Washington's a mess. The economy is uncertain. The ranks of the poor are growing larger. Our sense of morality is being questioned. Terrorism advances. You can look at any of it or all of it and say to yourself, *The world is going to pot.* And you can chat at coffee with your friends and say, What a shame. You can read and forward emails that claim that the world is going to be taken over by something or someone. You can blame every problem in America on one politician or another. And if you did any or all of that, people would consider you somewhat normal, just joining the ranks in the army of cynicism and pessimism.

But to claim the contrary opinion? To interject into the conversation that maybe God has something up his sleeve? To stop shaking your head and instead lay claim to the promises of God and to say, "Yeah, things aren't so hot, but God's not giving up, and I think he wants me to do something about it." Everybody these days seems to have a handle on the problem, or at least a loud opinion about it. But so few want to offer a solution. So few want to buy some land. So few want to lay claim to a redemptive deed. Lots of talk, little action.

Isn't that what Jeremiah has waving in his hand—a redemptive deed? It looks like just a deed to property, but it is a redemptive deed. A claim on the future. A parcel of hope.

A while ago I had the chance to go to St. Louis for a World Series game, and while I was there I had the chance to walk around downtown and came upon the Jefferson County Courthouse, where the fate of Dred Scott was handed down. You remember Dred Scott—the African American slave who in 1847, almost twenty years before the end of the Civil War, got up the gumption to sue for his freedom. Knowing that a good part of the white world at that time didn't see him nor his race as even being fully human, knowing that a good portion of his own people would see his suit for freedom not worth the trouble—in fact, making trouble—it was Dred Scott who looked into the future and saw hope. He looked into the future and wondered if the promises of God might be true. He saw a

God who promised never to let him or his people go. So in the face of scorn and ridicule and derision, the prophet sued for his freedom. And though the halls of justice denied Mr. and Mrs. Scott their claim to freedom and returned them to their owner, God's promises would still come true. Scott and his wife were subsequently freed by their owners, waving the redemptive deed not just to their own lives but to the lives of every fellow slave. God's promises would not be forgotten. And three years later Abraham Lincoln was elected president.

Jesus gathers his disciples at table in the face of an impending gloom. With the shadow of the cross lying heavy upon the assembled, Jesus lays claim to the future. He offers a down payment, saying that the world is not going to hell. He is putting his money where his mouth is. He is executing the redemptive deed. And he knows that from the foot of the cross they'll laugh and ridicule and deride and scorn—but such they did to the prophets who went before. But he, like they, know something that no one else knows. They see something that no one else can see: the Father who will not forget his promises, who will not let his children go.

So where, for God's sake, is the deed—the redemptive deed—of your life? Where, for God's sake, have you laid claim to the promised land? Where have you put yourself at risk—to say and to show that the promises of God are true and his purposes will not be denied? Where is the deed to the land that will someday be your children's? Your children's children? Your children's children's children?

Blessed are you who didn't give up. Blessed are you who laid claim to the future. Blessed are you who didn't give in to the cynicism. Blessed are you who bought a piece of property while everyone was leaving town. Blessed are you who endured the ridicule. Blessed are you who did battle with windmills. Rejoice and be glad, for your reward is great in heaven—for in the same way, they persecuted the prophets who were before you.

Too much sanity may be madness. And maddest of all: to see life as it is and not as it should be.

CHAPTER 21

The Empty Space

John 4:1–29

YEARS AGO THE SENIOR PASTOR of a large and prominent church in New York City—Riverside Church—stood before his congregation the Sunday following the death of his twenty-four-year-old son in a car accident and preached a sermon. William Sloane Coffin did what few preachers would attempt to do a week after their son's death—not just preach, but preach about the indescribable pain that such a death visits upon a person, and in particular, a parent. Some of you know of this pain. It is a fine sermon and worth finding on the Internet. It's called "Alex's Death."

I read it for the first time as a seminarian preparing myself to enter into the ministry of preaching, and when I read it I realized what Dr. Coffin was attempting to do. He bravely stood before his people that day because he wanted to teach them out of what had become for him, in an instant, an empty space. A space that had once been filled with a young, vibrant, energetic, fun-loving young son had now in the blink of an eye been left empty. He wanted to teach about the empty space. Not that he called it that, but that is what it was. And part of what Dr. Coffin reflected upon was the well-meaning effort of many to try to fill his empty space. People don't like empty spaces, their own nor others. Some tried to fill Dr. Coffin's empty space with pithy poems or dime-store theology. Some tried to fill it by explaining God's will. Some tried to fill it with Bible verses or platitudes. But Dr. Coffin that morning before his congregation of thousands was there to say that the empty space was not theirs to fill. It wasn't even his to fill.

Almost fifty years ago, N. W. Clerk wrote a tiny little book titled *A Grief Observed*. Published in England, it was a raw firsthand account of the penetrating grief of losing one's spouse. This man had lost his wife, and the ache was so deep that in the book he questions the presence of God. Where is God when it comes to my empty space? How could God leave me alone to deal with this pain? "When you are happy," he writes, "so happy that you have no sense needing [God], so happy that you are tempted to feel His claims upon you as an interruption, if you remember yourself and turn to Him with gratitude and praise, you will be—or so it feels—welcomed with open arms. But go to Him when your need is desperate, when all other help is vain, and what do you find? A door slammed in your face, and a sound of bolting and double bolting on the inside." Later he writes, "Talk to me about the truth of religion and I'll listen gladly. Talk to me about the duty of religion and I'll listen submissively. But don't come talking to me about the consolations of religion or I shall suspect you don't understand." He was speaking out of the empty space, this N. W. Clerk, which was discovered years later to be a pseudonym for C. S. Lewis. The real author's grief was the death of his wife, Joy. The real author's soul was an empty space that we cannot fill.

Not that we don't try. We try all kinds of things to fill the empty space. We try being busy. We try keeping active. We try an extra drink or two. We try mindless TV. We try eating too much or too little. We try giving advice. We all know the story of Job—the man who seemed to have it all, but before he knew it, everything was gone. His home, his family, his health. And Job was left alone with his empty space. Then come Job's "friends" and for thirty-five chapters they do their best to try to fill the empty space. They try to make sense of it all, to explain it all, to find blame and the reason for it all. But it's not working. The space is not getting filled. Then finally in the thirty-eighth chapter, God begins to speak into Job's empty space.

When I was a newly ordained pastor and installed in my first church in Philadelphia, I went to visit an elderly woman whose husband of fifty-five years had died just a few months before my arrival. I went to see how she was doing, because a few folks had told me she wasn't doing well. She invited me into her home and we talked for a while, and then she asked if I wanted to see Larry's room. Larry was her dead husband. Sure, I said. So she took me to Larry's study—and there it was, just as it was when Larry had died. Nothing touched. Nothing moved. It was her empty space. "I'm not ready," she said. I'm not sure what I exactly told her, but I know it was something trite like,

"Time heals all wounds"—some words that belied my youth and inexperience and discomfort with empty spaces. She patted my hand as if to say, "You don't understand." I visited her about once every three months, and each time she would show me the room unchanged—until a year or so later. Then, after we had talked awhile, she took me again to Larry's study and pointed out to me that the blanket on Larry's favorite chair was no longer there. She said, "I was sitting at breakfast the other day, and God spoke to me. He spoke into my empty space and said, 'It's time.' So now I'm starting. And I gave Larry's blanket to my grandson. Because Larry would have wanted that." With every visit afterward, she showed me another change—another way God had spoken into her empty space.

Jesus pays a visit to a well in the middle of Samaria—Jacob's Well—and he engages a Samaritan woman in a conversation. There are all sorts of cultural reasons why Jesus shouldn't be having this conversation with this Samaritan woman: men don't talk to women, Jews don't talk to Samaritans, and so on and so forth. But there Jesus is, speaking to this Samaritan woman. And they have this interesting conversation around water and buckets and living water and worship and spirit and truth and Jews and Samaritans, but in the middle of it all, Jesus tells her to go get her husband. She says that she has no husband. It's an awkward moment. And Jesus speaks into the awkward moment, saying, "I know. Truth is you've had five husbands, and the man you are living with now is not your husband." And now all of a sudden we see that this woman has an empty space. And the woman responds, "Sir, I see that you are a prophet."

The interesting thing about the empty space inside this woman is what history and tradition have tried to do to fill it. Jesus tells us that she has this empty space resulting from having been married several times and now is living with a man without benefit of marriage—and tradition has labeled her an immoral and loose woman. It's easy to fill someone else's empty space with that kind of label. Forget the cause; just call her a sinner. But what we keep forgetting is that a first-century Palestinian woman had no say in whom she was married to. She had no say in matters of divorce. That was the man's prerogative. Women were property to be claimed and discarded upon the man's whim. So this woman was either passed from one man to another or her husbands died along the way, and she had yet to find a man who would remain loyal. Her empty space, at the very least, was complicated and painful. It defied a label. For years she's come to the well alone, with no one who quite understands, and now in front of her was the one person who could see the situation for what it was and speak into it. The Jewish rabbi came to her not with labeling judgment but with the grace of living water . . . to fill not the bucket in her hand but the dry well inside her soul. The empty space.

Jesus said, "Blessed are those who mourn, for they shall be comforted." Blessed? Did he say "blessed"? We must be careful to know that Jesus does not wish the empty space upon us. Love would never do that. It's just that he knows that to be a human being we all walk around with a "God-shaped vacuum," as Pascal called it. We all have a place that has been left empty by disappointment or failure or death or illness or hurt. We all have that room inside us where we go to mourn. We all have that space that is desperate for comfort, and Jesus says that comfort will come. God will someday speak into the space. Maybe not today or tomorrow or next month, but God loves you enough to speak into the dry well inside you with an invitation of living water—water that will quench the thirst of your parched soul. And it is likely not going to feel like a Hallmark card or anything else we expect. But God will speak in spirit and truth a word that will inhabit that space and in God's mysterious and surprising way will bring comfort.

Blessed are those who trust that. Blessed are those who wait for that. Blessed are those who resist the temptation to fill the space—yours or someone else's—with something that tries to bring false comfort through a trite formula.

Don Wardlaw, a retired professor from McCormick Seminary, tells the story of going to his father's funeral. His father was a Presbyterian minister, so at the funeral were lots of folks who came to tell Don what his father's ministry had meant to them. One of them was the custodian who had once worked for his father. The man had moved away but had returned for the funeral. He came to Don and said, "Your dad was very important and special to me."

"Oh, I know, Leon; you were very important to him."

"No, no . . . you don't understand," said Leon. "I wouldn't be here today if it weren't for your dad. I wouldn't have made it through that horrible night."

"What horrible night?" Don asked.

"During the time that your dad was pastor of this church and he and I worked together here, you probably don't remember this because you were a little boy, but my wife died suddenly. She was only thirty-four years old. She was hanging out clothes on the line. She had a massive heart attack. She didn't even make it to the hospital alive. We had four small kids. I will never forget that day. I was just devastated. I was so emotionally drained that I fell across the bed. I remember lying in the bed and it had gotten dark. I looked up at one point, and I could see your dad had come into the room and was sitting in a rocking chair beside my bed, rocking. He didn't say a thing. He just sat there rocking. All night long I would wake up and I would reach over to where my wife usually was, and I would feel that emptiness. The pain would shoot through me like a thousand arrows. And I wondered how in the world can I go on? And then out of the corner of my eye I would see him rocking, rocking. It was the rocking that helped me make it through the night."

Blessed are those who mourn, for they shall be comforted.

The Gospel According to Baseball

CHAPTER 22

The Friendly Confines

—ᴧᴧᴧ—

1 Corinthians 11:23–34

C. S. Lewis, in his book *Surprised by Joy*, relates the story of his younger life and his journey toward a belief in God. In the opening pages of his account, he tells of what he can remember to be his first experience of something he calls *sehnsucht*. *Sehnsucht* is a German word that Lewis believes captures most the experience he had as a young boy when he encountered for the first time something strikingly beautiful. It was something as simple as a toy garden that his brother had made, but the young Lewis seeing it for the first time was so struck by its sense of beauty that in the moment he experienced a sense of longing—a yearning for something beyond what the beauty represented. That's what *sehnsucht* means—longing—a longing that comes from a moment of the sublime that goes as quickly as it comes and makes us long for the joy that for a moment we experienced in this encounter with beauty. Through the rest of the story, Lewis points to many of these experiences of longing that came from his brushes with beauty—whether a pastoral vista, a Wagnerian opera, or a touching poem—whatever it might be that quickened joy and made him long for the source from which the joy came. These were important experiences for Lewis on his way to finding God.

I can imagine that you have also had those kinds of experiences in your life, encounters with beauty and wonder that make you long for that sense of joy that only comes to us in fleeting moments of time and space. Just a few nights ago I stepped outside my house and looked up into the cloudless Florida night sky, and all I could see was a sea of stars. Stars everywhere, and it was so beautiful and overwhelming that it gave me a stab of joy. But almost as quickly as the joy came, it went, leaving me longing.

Dr. John Sexton, president of New York University, in his compelling book *Baseball as a Road to God*, speaks of this sense of longing in a different way when he points us to the work of twentieth-century French philosopher Mircea Eliade. Eliade in his study of religion focused on the experience humans have of the sacred—places where we experience, in a deeply personal way, the touch of the transcendent. Eliade calls these experiences of the sacred *hierophany*. To experience hierophany is to come to a place and time where there is a deep sense of sacredness. A holy ground. Something that points us to a thing not visible, but perhaps more real.

This happens to me whenever I visit the battlefields of Gettysburg. Gettysburg in one sense is simply a little town in central Pennsylvania, surrounded by rolling hills of farmland, that at first glance is no different than any other little town in Pennsylvania. But to know what happened there—how many men died there, what speech was given there—is to sense in those rolling fields a holy ground, a sense of the sacred. One is transported to a transcendent plane. Life takes on a gravity there. According to Eliade, "Where the sacred manifests itself in space, the real unveils itself."

You can, I'm sure, bring to mind some places you would call sacred. The nave of a cathedral. A wooded path. A quiet beach. A favorite meeting place. These become holy grounds, places where we touch the transcendent.

Sexton goes on to say that, for baseball fans such as himself, one such sacred space is a baseball stadium. In a baseball stadium, fans are brought back in touch with a game that they likely met when they were young. Mom or Dad or a brother or sister took them to the local ball field and played catch or hit grounders or engaged in a game of pickle. And from there it was the Little League games played with uniforms and coaches and scorecards—and then eventually it was the first trip to a professional baseball stadium, where they (we) were overwhelmed by the brilliant green grass and the combed dirt and the bright white lines and the walls and outfield stands a million miles away. And our return to such places puts us back in touch with something deeper and bigger . . . a brush with joy that makes us long for the sense of the real that lies beyond the beauty. Some would call it a longing for the past or a longing for simpler times or a longing for the relationships of our youth.

There are a thousand reasons why the United States calls baseball its national pastime. Something about this game puts it on the short list of things essentially American, along with Mom and apple pie.

A lot of this gets captured in a movie that came out a couple of decades ago, *Field of Dreams.* Whenever I am asked to name my favorite movies, invariably *Field of Dreams* is at the top of the list. Generally I am not a sports movie kind of guy, but *Field of Dreams*, whenever I watch it, does a number on me. Many of you have seen it. It's about a husband and wife who purchase a farm in Iowa and there they raise their daughter and acres and acres of corn. Then one day Ray, the husband, hears a voice that tells him to build a baseball field on his farm. Plow under a few acres of corn and construct a beautiful baseball field complete with lights, stands, backstop, you name it. He does. And as a result all these legends from a bygone era of baseball show up to play: Gil Hodges, Smokey Joe Wood, Shoeless Joe Jackson. They walk out of the cornfields to play baseball again. Ray and his family get to witness all this. At one point he travels around the country and brings back to the field those who, for whatever reason, have a longing to connect with the game and with the heroes of yesteryear. But the decision to plow under his corn and build this field was not, in itself, a prudent economic decision, and Ray at one point faces foreclosure on the property. He is sorely tempted to sell the property and give up this amazing, somewhat supernatural experience of the return of baseball's greats. As he contemplates this decision, one of those he has gathered to bring to his field, an author named Terence Mann, stands and imagines that there will come a day when people from all over America will want to come and visit this field of dreams. And then he delivers a monologue about baseball and its pull on the American soul. He imagines people arriving to the middle of Iowa and pictures what they will do:

> And they'll walk off to the bleachers and sit in their short sleeves on a perfect afternoon. And find they have reserved seats somewhere along the baselines where they sat when they were children. And cheer their heroes. And they'll watch the game, and it'll be as they'd dipped themselves in magic waters. The memories will be so thick, they'll have to brush them away from their faces. People will come, Ray. The one constant through all the years, Ray, has been baseball. America has rolled by like an army of steamrollers. It's been erased like a blackboard, rebuilt and erased again. But baseball has marked the time. This field, this game, is a part of our past, Ray. It reminds us of all that once was good, and that could be again.

So what is it about baseball that would cause it to endure, to make it America's pastime, to be the topic of movies, the arena of childhood heroes, the subject of monologues, the theme of poems, a mythology handed down from generation to generation? What do we long for when we step onto a diamond or into the centerfield stands?

Baseball, at its core, is changeless, isn't it? Apart from the occasional tweak to an occasional rule, it is a changeless institution. At whatever point in time that baseball was invented—and there is great debate over who really invented baseball and when it happened—the game was established with its four bases ninety feet apart and its pitching mound sixty feet, six inches from home plate and its foul lines that extend as far as you want to extend them and its four balls and three strikes and its three outs and nine innings and its gloves and bats and singles and doubles and triples and home runs and its walks and strikeouts—all those things that even if you are not a baseball fan you probably know a little about. For this institution of throwing, catching, and hitting—that has made farm boys into heroes and superstars into goats—the constitution of the game has changed very little. Go back not to just the last century but to the century before that—and it's still three strikes, you're out . . . three outs and you're in the field, and nine innings given to both teams to score more runs than the other. Baseball is a changeless game.

Roger Angell, some thirty years ago in the *New Yorker*, wrote of how he had the chance to attend a college baseball game up at Yale to watch Yale's star pitcher—a kid named Ron Darling. And while watching he was seated next to Smokey Joe Wood, the pitcher who almost single-handedly won the World Series for the Red Sox in 1912. There Angell sat—next to a ninety-year-old star watching a twenty-year-old star—and they were stars of the same game. Nothing had changed.

We long for changeless institutions, don't we? Baseball is changeless.

As well, baseball is a game of many and equal chances. Each gets as many chances as the others. Each gets three strikes. Each gets three outs. Each gets nine innings. No one gets to say that they didn't have a chance. It doesn't matter if you are inside the friendly confines of Wrigley or the House That Ruth Built or the dome of Tropicana or the sandlot behind the grade school—every field and stadium is different, each with its own character. But once you're inside and the lines are drawn and the bases are placed and the bats are put out and the stitched ball is located, then everyone knows what the game is about—a game anyone can play, and everyone has a chance. And nothing about it (I hope) will change until the end of time.

We long for institutions like that, don't we? Simple in their structure, enduring in their very nature, and inclusive in their chances.

Could we say these things about what we do here under this dome? Could we say this about the church, an institution created so very long ago—long enough to make baseball look like a game invented yesterday? Could we say that what we attempt here has within it its own simplicity, its own grand history, its own nature of inclusivity? Anyone can play this game. Everyone gets a chance here. Go from coast to coast, and you will not find one church that looks like the other, at least not exactly. Clear window, stained windows. Georgian clapboard, colonial redbrick, Gothic sandstone, corporate conference center, vaulted nave, Shaker meeting—it all looks so different on the outside—as different as Fenway is from Marlins Stadium is from Riverview High. But when you get down to it—like the lines and bases of every diamond in America—the church has its own changeless markings and touchstones. Pulpit, table, font. Word and sacrament. Some things are changeless, and some things are endless in their chances.

It's what the apostle Paul was trying to get across to the Corinthians—that early church that was trying to make the gospel a lot more complicated than it needed to be. Arguments took place over who had the better gifts, what kind of food they could eat, what morality they should practice, and in the middle of Paul's response to these confused and complicated people, he institutes for them the Lord's Supper. He repeats the words of Christ and says it is as simply as this: Word and sacrament. One Lord, one faith, one baptism. This is what will last. You can have your programs and your building campaigns and your fund drives and your committee meetings, but the enduring institution is what takes place at pulpit, table, and font. "The marks of the true church," Calvin wrote, "are that the Word of God should be preached, and that the sacraments be rightly administered." This is what people will come back to, tying them to the generations before and after. These are the lines and bases. Anyone can play here. All have their chances here. And though the church from generation to generation falls in and out of favor—though there are times when the whole thing seems irrelevant to one age or another—the human longing never goes away. The hunger for hierophany remains. The sacred space is always yearned for.

It explains to me the elder to whom I was once talking. He told me of a time when life was falling apart. Family troubles. Difficulties at work. Financial worries. Life had jolted him. His way home from work would take him past a church, a simple little Georgian white clapboard that had been there since the end of the Civil War. He said that just about every day when he approached the church driving his car, he would slow down and pull to the side. And for a minute or two he'd just sit and look. The steeple. The windows. The enduring building in which hundreds had been baptized, including his own. Thousands fed at table. Thousands fed from pulpit. And peace, he said, would invariably come as he considered all of what such walls had housed. The eternal. The sacred place.

This is what we are—the church. In season or out of season. The gathered who bring their longings, yearning to be met by something real. Something that doesn't change. Lines and bases. Pulpit, table, font. Believing that it can happen over and over in such friendly confines.

CHAPTER 23

Bases Covered

Micah 6:6–8

Wee Willie Keeler, a right fielder who played for an assortment of professional baseball teams at the turn of the twentieth century—Baltimore, Boston, New York—was at the time—and for all time—one of the greatest hitters in the game. With a career batting average of .341, twelfth best in history, he was the preeminent placement hitter—versatile enough that he could swing and get the ball where he wanted it in the field. When asked the secret to being a good hitter, Wee Willie Keeler coined the phrase, "Hit 'em where they ain't."

Hit 'em where they ain't.

It may be the most practical and obvious tip in baseball. And if that is the case, then the inverse is perhaps just as true. A good defense in baseball—the best way to keep the opposing team from scoring runs—is to be where the ball is, to put yourself in position for where the ball is likely going to go. To cover your part of the field. To be at your particular base.

In baseball, hitting is always going to take the headlines, but it can reasonably be said that perhaps just as many games have been won or lost because of what took place or didn't take place out in the field. Lefty Gomez, the great Hall of Fame pitcher, once stated that the secret to his success was "clean living and a fast outfield."

The positions on a baseball field are laid out to defend against the law of averages. Players are placed strategically to account for the greatest opportunity to snag a ground ball, fly ball, bunted ball, or screaming liner. And the trick about fielding is how a team adjusts its positions. When a left-handed hitter is at the plate, the defense will likely shift a little to the right because left-handed hitters tend to hit to the right. When a right-handed hitter bats, the players will shift a little to the left.

Some baseball analysts claim that the 1946 World Series between the St. Louis Cardinals and the Boston Red Sox was won and lost not by what took place at the bat, but what took place in the field. That Series featured the greatest hitter in the game at that time, Ted Williams. Ted Williams was a left-handed hitter and could be counted on to hit the ball almost exclusively to the right side of the field. St. Louis employed a shift when Williams came to the plate, called the Williams shift. They shifted the third baseman to play between the shortstop and the second baseman—so sure were they that Williams would hit to the right. They were correct, and Williams had a terrible World Series, getting only five hits and one run batted in, unable to hit it where they ain't. The Cardinals put themselves where they knew the ball would be. Ironically, it was late in the seventh game of the World Series when the Red Sox were in the field that a substitute in center field for the Red Sox, Leon Culberson, did not position himself correctly to be ready for Harry Walker's loop single that allowed Enos Slaughter to score all the way from first base and win the Series. It took almost sixty years for Boston to win a World Series after that—against the Cardinals, oddly enough, in 2004.

All of this is to say that one of the keys to good baseball is being where you need to be, putting yourself in the best place to get to where the ball will be. Every time a ball is hit, every player moves to where they will be needed most. A ground ball to first base means the pitcher runs and covers first. A single to right field means the second baseman runs to shallow right to take the relay while the shortstop covers second. A batter shows bunt, and the third and first basemen charge the line while the second baseman covers first and the shortstop covers third. Every player needs to be where he needs to be. All bases need to be covered. One of the great sins in baseball is not to be where you need to be.

Interesting thing about baseball: you can fail at the plate two-thirds of the time and be considered a hitting phenom, but if you fail in the field more than 2 or 3 percent of the time, they'll likely send you to the minors.

For ten years the Chicago Cubs employed one of the great double-play combinations: shortstop Joe Tinker, second baseman Johnny Evers, and first baseman Frank Chance. With a runner on first and a ground ball hit to the shortstop, the Cubs announcer would call it, "Tinker to Evers to Chance." Each man in the place he needed to be. So long did this double-play combination last that they even commemorated it with a poem:

> These are the saddest of possible words:
> "Tinker to Evers to Chance."
> Trio of bear cubs, and fleeter than birds,
> Tinker and Evers and Chance.
> Ruthlessly pricking our gonfalon bubble,
> Making a Giant hit into a double—
> Words that are heavy with nothing but trouble:
> "Tinker to Evers to Chance."

And, of course, who can forget good ol' Abbott and Costello trying to sort out, "Who's on first, What's on second, and I don't know is on third"?

Baseball is about being where you need to be, ensuring that all the bases are covered.

Life is a journey of discovering how to cover the bases. "Have you covered your bases?" is a familiar question that we have been asked since we were young. Life is all about the preparation, doing what needs to be done. "Have you cleaned your plate?" we were asked at the dinner table. "Have you brushed your teeth?" we heard at bedtime. "Have you studied for your test?" we were grilled on our way to school. "Have you combed your hair?"—on the way to our first date. "Have you shined your shoes?"—before the big interview. Have you covered your bases?

Later in life it's questions like, "Have you enough for retirement . . . the right insurance?" "Have you made out a will?" "Have you made peace with the people in your life?"

Have you covered the bases? Have you put yourself where you need to be? Are you ready to receive whatever life has to throw at you?

At one level this question about covering your bases is very Darwinian. Survival of the fittest. Only the strongest survive. And when thinking about our bases being covered, we consider ourselves and our family. Covering your bases has always been about protecting yourself. Have you put yourself in the right position—to take care of you? Or to take care of your household? Nothing wrong about that, I suppose. We all need food and shelter. But remember the story from way back in the first chapter of this book? Jesus tells us the story about the coming of the bridegroom for the wedding and the question of whether the bridesmaids will be ready with their lit lanterns to greet him? It's Jesus' way of asking, Will we be ready for the advent of the kingdom? Will we have our bases covered for the arrival of the Messiah? Is your lantern lit, not for yourself, but for someone else? And it seems we have maidens who have their bases covered and those who don't—those who have their lanterns full of oil for the kingdom and those who don't. You can be all dressed up, Jesus says, but with no place to go. Because you haven't covered your bases.

So what is it all about? What does it mean to have your bases covered when it comes to the kingdom of heaven?

Well, it would seem, as one takes a look from Genesis to Revelation, that the Bible echoes over and over a refrain on preparation. Maybe it is summed up best in Micah's great rhetorical question: What does the Lord require of you? How do I make sure I have my bases covered when it comes to the Lord? Where do I need to be to be ready for whatever life might throw at me? Is it the right insurance plan? Is it the right number in my 401(k)? Is it a certain amount of money in the offering plate? Is it the right score on my SAT? What bases does the Lord look to have covered when it comes to the living of our days?

He has told you, O mortal—says the prophet. It's already there in the Law. It's already there in the Prophets. The bases are clear to see. What are we to make sure we cover? To do justice. To love kindness. To walk humbly with our God. First base. Second base. Third base. Where do you want to be when the ball is in play? You want to be covering your bases. You want to be doing justice, you want to be loving all things kind, you want to be humble in your walk. These are the things we must be prepared for.

Life can throw a lot of things at us. We all know that. Life throws its fortune and its misfortune. The rain falls on the just and the unjust. But what does the Lord require? Every man out for himself? Dog eat dog? To each his own? No, whatever life should throw is always to be met with justice, kindness, and humility.

Every day is different. Every year is different. Every age is different. Who is to know what time and history will throw at us? What changes will occur? What circumstances will arise? What ball will be in play? "Every man to his post," is what Churchill said to the British people as they waited for what seemed to be the inevitable invasion of the Nazis. Every man to his post—and it wasn't just the military to whom he was speaking. It was every citizen. The home guard protecting the streets. The night watchmen. The homemakers making do with rationed supplies. Children praying. Every man to his post. Every player to his base.

In the bleak days of American slavery, when people of African descent were seeking to escape their bondage, many came to rely upon the Underground Railroad, stations along the way where fugitives to freedom could hide from the law. And each of those stations was the simple home or barn or loft of an American citizen who, when the knock came to the door and the opportunity arose to risk a life to do justice and love kindness, humbly put their households at risk to make sure that when it came to the kingdom, their base would be covered. They had taken up their post. Living awhile in Philadelphia, we came to learn of one William Still, a freed African American living in that city in the mid-nineteenth century who knew that the times had called for him to be one such stop on the Railroad—one such hiding place, one such respite on the journey to freedom—to shepherd people to what they called back then the "Promised Land": Canada. Hundreds came his way, each bringing the risk of imprisonment, even a return to slavery. They were perilous times. And when later in life William Still was asked about his participation in the Underground, he responded, "It was my good fortune to lend a helping hand to the weary travelers flying from the land of bondage."

Good fortune? Good fortune to put you and those you loved at such great risk? Good fortune to be living in such harrowing times? Good fortune to focus your life on making life better for others? Good fortune to do justice, love kindness, walk humbly? Well, of course—for that is the point of the game, isn't it? To make sure the right bases are covered. To be where you need to be when the ball is in play.

It just so happened that two important men died in the same week recently. Maybe not important to us, but important to a good many. Will Campbell died this week. If you were a civil rights worker in the fifties and sixties you knew that Will Campbell, a Baptist preacher, was the only white preacher whom anyone in the civil rights leadership knew they could trust, the only one invited to be a part of the Southern Christian Leadership Conference. Why? Because Will Campbell knew that it wasn't the color of your skin that was to determine whether you were responsible for justice. If your neighbor was in trouble, it was every man to his post, every player to his base. Whether it was escorting nine black high school students to the all-white Central High School in Little Rock or sitting at a lunch counter or marching in the local civil rights march, Will Campbell covered his bases well—to the scorn of many of his white brothers and sisters. It was his good fortune.

Bob Fletcher also died. He had been an agricultural inspector for the state of California back during World War II. That's when the government began to round up Japanese

Americans into internment camps. These were the people he knew, people he serviced. Mr. Fletcher was approached by a Japanese American farmer. Was there something he could do to help? Well, no. He couldn't prevent his friends from being taken from their homes, but there was something he could do. He could quit his job and, to the chagrin of many of his friends and neighbors, he could take over three of the farms of his Japanese neighbors while they were interred. He could raise their crops, working eighteen hours a day. He could pay their mortgages and their taxes, and he could cover his expenses and leave his exiled friends half the profits in the bank when they got home. Yes, that's what he could do. He could cover those bases. Why, it would be his good fortune to do so.

And yours? What might your good fortune be? What base might you be pleased to cover? It will be different for each of us. The ball is in play at different places in the field, but the bases remain the same. Do justice. Love kindness. Walk humbly. Plenty of opportunities that each of our histories present. We're all in different places and different times in life. Each of us resides in a different circumstance. But the fortune remains the same. The good fortune to hear the voice of the master, "Well done, good and faithful servant. Well done, William Still. Well done, Will Campbell. Well done, Bob Fletcher . . . for when the ball was in play, you covered the bases."

CHAPTER 24

Swing Away

Matthew 25:14–30

The outlook wasn't brilliant for the Mudville nine that day:
The score stood four to two, with but one inning more to play.
And then when Cooney died at first, and Barrows did the same,
A sickly silence fell upon the patrons of the game.
A straggling few got up to go in deep despair. The rest
Clung to that hope which springs eternal in the human breast;
They thought, if only Casey could get but a whack at that—
We'd put up even money, now, with Casey at the bat.
But Flynn preceded Casey, as did also Jimmy Blake,
And the former was a lulu and the latter was a cake;
So upon that stricken multitude grim melancholy sat,
For there seemed but little chance of Casey's getting to the bat.
But Flynn let drive a single, to the wonderment of all,
And Blake, the much despis-ed, tore the cover off the ball;
And when the dust had lifted, and the men saw what had occurred,
There was Jimmy safe at second and Flynn a-hugging third.

Then from 5,000 throats and more there rose a lusty yell;
It rumbled through the valley, it rattled in the dell;
It knocked upon the mountain and recoiled upon the flat,
For Casey, mighty Casey, was advancing to the bat.
There was ease in Casey's manner as he stepped into his place;
There was pride in Casey's bearing and a smile on Casey's face.
And when, responding to the cheers, he lightly doffed his hat,
No stranger in the crowd could doubt 'twas Casey at the bat.
Ten thousand eyes were on him as he rubbed his hands with dirt;
Five thousand tongues applauded when he wiped them on his shirt.
Then while the writhing pitcher ground the ball into his hip,
Defiance gleamed in Casey's eye, a sneer curled Casey's lip.
And now the leather-covered sphere came hurtling through the air,
And Casey stood a-watching it in haughty grandeur there.
Close by the sturdy batsman the ball unheeded sped—
"That ain't my style," said Casey. "Strike one," the umpire said.
From the benches, black with people, there went up a muffled roar,
Like the beating of the storm-waves on a stern and distant shore.
"Kill him! Kill the umpire!" shouted someone on the stand;
And its likely they'd a-killed him had not Casey raised his hand.
With a smile of Christian charity great Casey's visage shone;
He stilled the rising tumult; he bade the game go on;
He signaled to the pitcher, and once more the spheroid flew;
But Casey still ignored it, and the umpire said, "Strike two."
"Fraud!" cried the maddened thousands, and echo answered fraud;
But one scornful look from Casey and the audience was awed.
They saw his face grow stern and cold, they saw his muscles strain,

And they knew that Casey wouldn't let that ball go by again.
The sneer is gone from Casey's lip, his teeth are clenched in hate;
He pounds with cruel violence his bat upon the plate.
And now the pitcher holds the ball, and now he lets it go,
And now the air is shattered by the force of Casey's blow.
Oh, somewhere in this favored land the sun is shining bright;
The band is playing somewhere, and somewhere hearts are light,
And somewhere men are laughing, and somewhere children shout;
But there is no joy in Mudville—mighty Casey has struck out.

If anyone should doubt the place that baseball holds in American culture, one need only recite that poem by Ernest Thayer to know that the story of baseball is at some level the story of us all. The epic battle between pitcher and batter and umpire and crowd is a mythology written over and over again in each of our lives. As I write, this month marks the 125th anniversary of Thayer's poem, which has as its original title, "Casey at the Bat: A Ballad of the Republic Sung in 1888." *A ballad of the Republic.*

Lots can be said about this poem, but I suppose in the end it's a simple story of the chance a batter gets at the plate. In the ninth inning for the Mudville nine, five batters get their chance at the plate. Five batters get their chance to help their team come back from a two-run deficit, maybe even to win the game. Five batters are each given the chance to swing at at least three pitches, maybe more, and to put the ball in play and to hit 'em where they ain't and to get themselves on base, or better yet, to clear the bases with a home run. It doesn't matter what pitcher you're facing—David Price, Mariano Rivera, Nolan Ryan, the local Little League southpaw—the guy on the mound is obligated to present you with three pitches in the strike zone to swing at, and it's your job as the batter to swing. You can pray and hope for a walk. You can pray and hope that the pitcher is a little wild and that four balls will not make their way to the strike zone and you are given a free pass to first base. That can be your hope and that can be your prayer, but that's not what baseball is about. No player worth his salt plays the game that way. In fact, if you receive a walk in baseball, it's considered a nonevent, not an at-bat. It puts you on first, but it is a statistical nothing. In baseball you are supposed to go up and take your licks.

When I was a boy I used to love watching a player named Manny Sanguillen bat. Manny Sanguillen was a catcher for the Pittsburgh Pirates, and there was not a pitch thrown to Manny that Manny did not like. He was what was called a bad-ball hitter. Pitchers didn't have to worry much about getting the ball too close to the plate because Manny was going to swing at it. He rarely walked. Six seasons of over 475 plate appearances, and Manny Sanguillen walked no more than twenty-two times in any of those seasons. "The way to fool Manny Sanguillen," said one opposing coach, "is to throw him [a pitch] right down the middle. He'll hit anything but a perfect pitch."

The truth is that life very seldom throws us a perfect pitch. Having said that, though, I am reminded of the story of when Mickey Mantle batted for the last time in Detroit's Tiger Stadium. Pitcher Denny McLain had already won thirty games that season, and the Tigers had the game well in hand. McLain got the message to Mantle through his catcher, Jim Price, that he was going to give him a chance to hit a home run in his last at-bat in Detroit—to throw him a perfect pitch. "What pitch do you want?" the catcher asked Mantle. Mantle told him the pitch he wanted and that's the pitch McLain gave him, and Mantle hit the ball into the upper deck. But you and I are not Mickey Mantle, and you and I seldom get a perfect pitch to hit. Life throws its curveballs. That's what we say, isn't it—when the unexpected happens, when the unfortunate circumstance arrives? "I just got thrown a curveball." I got less than a perfect pitch. But life is not about waiting around for the perfect pitch, because likely it will never come. Life is about swinging away.

I have to admit that there are enough fiscally conservative bones in my body that when I read the story that Jesus tells in Matthew 25 of the three servants who are given a varying amount of dollars to invest—that's what talents were: currency, dollars—that I find there to be upon first reading little fault in the one-talent servant who decides not to risk, like the others do, investing his money out of fear that he might lose it and have nothing to return to the master when he gets back. It's hard for me at first to understand the anger of the master when he hears of those dollars being buried. *Sure,* I want to say to myself, *it's fine that the other two made a killing in the market, but what would have happened if they had lost it all? What would the master have said then? Wouldn't the one- talent guy become the hero?* I ask myself. "Well done, good and faithful servant. While the market was crashing, you put your money under your mattress! You held the bat on your shoulders and waited for a walk!"

Of course, that's not the point of the story. The point of the story is to grasp what life is about. Life is not about perfect market conditions. Life is not about a guaranteed bull market. Life is not about a sure bet. Life is not about waiting for the perfect pitch. Life is about swinging away, trying to put your bat to the ball even if the pitch is high and outside, finding your inner Manny Sanguillen.

I love the story that Tim McCarver tells about catching for Bob Gibson, the great Cardinals pitcher. At one point in one game McCarver went walking to the mound to chat with Gibson about an upcoming batter, and halfway there Gibson yelled to him, "Turn around and go back, McCarver. The only thing you know about pitching is that it's hard to hit."

Pitching is hard to hit and living is hard to live. And when you feel in life like you are standing sixty feet, six inches away from a hundred-mile-an-hour fastballer, the temptation is to keep your bat on your shoulders. Bury your talent in the ground. Hope for a benign walk to first. That's what the master was trying to say to the cowardly servant: better to go down swinging than to be caught looking. To be caught looking is perhaps the worst sin of batting—to let a hittable pitch pass you by. Good ol' Casey struck out because he gave himself only one chance to swing. He got caught looking at the other two. Going down swinging is not the worst thing that can happen in the kingdom of baseball, nor in the kingdom of heaven. Reggie Jackson, one of the great home-run hitters of all time, struck out five times for every home run he hit. They still called him Mr. October.

The truth is that you can spend a lot of time debating lots of things about the nature of our existence. You can talk a lot about where we came from and how life was formed. You can talk about creation and evolution. You can talk about who's right and who's wrong on this issue or that issue—but the crux of the matter really is what are you going to do now that you're at the plate? For whatever reason, life has you up at the plate. You got your three pitches; what are you going to do with them? Are you going to talk about it . . . or are you going to swing the bat? Are you going to let your fear of a strikeout keep you from swinging for the fences?

In Shakespeare's *Measure for Measure* Isabella is pressed upon to intercede for her brother who is unjustly sentenced to execution for a minor crime, and she wonders what good she can do against the powers that be. Lucio's rejoinder is, "Our doubts are traitors, and make us lose the good we oft might win, by fearing to attempt." It's the same message that Queen Esther receives from her brother Mordecai when she is given the chance to intercede with the bloodthirsty king for her people who are at grave risk. Queen Esther is deathly afraid to appeal to the king for clemency for her people—and her brother says to her, "Who knows? Perhaps you have come to royal dignity for such a time as this?" In other words, it's your time at the plate. Your greatest risk is not to strike out, but to be caught looking. *Our doubts are traitors, and make us lose the good we oft might win, by fearing to attempt.*

Maybe that's a part of what Jesus was saying when he said that the one who loses his life is the one who will gain it. That is to say, the one who loses his fear of losing his life is the one who really gets his life. The one who loses his fear of striking out is the one who swings the hardest. And the one who swings the hardest is the one most bound to clear the fence.

There is a big world out there to make a difference in. Do justice. Love kindness. Walk humbly. We can do lots of good if we are willing to swing. Not much good we can do with the bat on our shoulders watching the next best reality show on TV. Friends, the best reality show right now is the one with you up to the plate. You. Right now. And the "great cloud of witnesses" is up in the stands waiting for Casey at the Bat. Larry at the Bat. Sally at the Bat. Tony at the Bat. Mallory at the Bat. Each of us gets our pitches. Some are fast. Some are curves. Some are knuckleballs. Some are in the dirt. And some are under our chins. But the great cloud of witnesses is looking to see what we might do with our at-bat.

What will it be? Wait, pray, and hope for a walk? Or will the air be shattered by the force of our blow?

CHAPTER 25

My Kingdom for a Bunt

—∞—

Mark 12:41–44

C. S. Lewis, in one of his great essays, "The World's Last Night"—an essay about our consideration and sometimes over-consideration of the Second Coming of Jesus—makes a point that our lives are lived like characters in a play. And when you are a character in a play or a story, because you are in the story you have no idea necessarily how and when the story will end. When you are a character in a play you don't necessarily know what act you are in: first, third, or fifth. The actor, of course, knows, but not the character. And Lewis makes the point that the key to life is not knowing the whens and the hows of the end—when the curtain will fall. The key to life is what you do when it's your time out on the stage. You may be the lead character or you may play a bit part, but the key is what your role is and how you are playing it.

To illustrate this matter, Lewis points us to a scene in Shakespeare's great *King Lear*. It is the middle of the third act.

Treachery is afoot, and the Earl of Gloucester is being undermined by his own flesh and blood. A servant of the earl who observes this betrayal and an attack on his master jumps to the fore and seeks to defend his lord. He brandishes a sword, utters no more than eight lines, but before he can do much good, he is stabbed in the back by the king's daughter. That is his whole part on the stage—the loyal defense of his lord. So minor a character is he that Shakespeare gives him no name. But Lewis reminds us that in the precious time this small character had the stage—not knowing even what act he was in or when the curtain would fall—he played his part well. He responded to the call. He sacrificed himself for the cause. "We do not know the play," Lewis writes. "We do not even know whether we are in Act I or Act V. We do not know who are the major and who are the minor characters. The Author knows. . . . [And] we are led to expect that the Author will have something to say to each of us on the part that each of us has played. The playing it well is what matters infinitely."

The Author will have something to say to each of us on the part that each of us has played. The playing it well is what matters infinitely.

There are lots of parts to be played on a baseball diamond, too. There are pitchers and catchers. There are runners and batters. There are fielders and coaches. Everyone has their part to perform, their position to play. The mechanics of baseball, like most team sports, from a distance look very simple. Throw, catch, and hit. What could be so hard about that? But baseball is a game about how well you do the little things, whether you paid attention to the things in which maybe most fans from a distance have little interest.

Leo Durocher, that great theologian, once said, "Baseball is like church—many attend, few understand." Spoken like a true manager, who while everyone is focused on the slugger at the plate, he has to worry about who will be batting two innings later. Who will be coming onto the stage in act 3, or inning 5? The manager understands that it's often the bit part, and how well the bit part is played, that determines whether you win the game.

One of those bit parts—unique to baseball—is the sacrifice bunt. The sacrifice bunt takes place when a runner is on first, or runners are on first and second, and the manager wants those runners to be in scoring position. The manager tells the batter to bunt the ball down the first or third baseline so that the runners can advance. When successful in his sacrifice bunt, the batter is usually thrown out at first. He sacrifices himself in order to advance the runners so that they are in better position to score on a future base hit. Pitchers are often asked to sacrifice bunt—unless you are from the apostate American League, which polluted the game with the designated hitter forty years ago.

From a distance, laying down a sacrifice bunt doesn't appear to be that difficult. Just square your bat—let the ball hit the bat so that the ball trickles down the line and the runners get their chance to advance. Players are taught this in Little League. And yet how often we see a player getting paid the gross national product of a small country stride to the plate, square himself . . . and he cannot bunt the ball. He cannot advance the runners. He cannot extend the inning for the team. "My kingdom," many managers have uttered to themselves, "for a bunt."

Only in baseball do they have a play called a sacrifice. Only in baseball after a bunt is properly laid and a player sacrifices himself and he trots back to the bench after being called out at first does the team stand to congratulate him—because he has done a very important and strategic thing for the team: He has advanced the runners. He has helped the team. He has made it possible for others, not himself, to score. Because in baseball it doesn't matter *who* scores; what matters is that *the team* scores. Interesting, isn't it, that one of the lesser valued individual statistics in baseball is personal runs scored. You are more important to the team if you have the ability to bat other players in than to score yourself.

The late Mario Cuomo, former governor of New York and former professional baseball player signed at the same time as Mickey Mantle for twice as much money, once said that baseball "is a community activity. You need all nine people helping one another. I love bunt plays. I love the idea of the bunt. I love the idea of the sacrifice. Even the word is good. Giving yourself up for the good of the whole. That's Jeremiah. That's thousands of years of wisdom. You find your own good in the good of the whole. You find your own individual fulfillment in the success of the community—the Bible tried to do that and didn't teach you. Baseball did."

I suppose that's part of what Jesus was trying to say when he noticed the parade of folks placing their offerings at the temple treasury. The rich folks were bringing their big checks, and it's all well and good and lots of help will be given—and everyone will know that they are the ones scoring the runs and making the headlines. But Jesus—like the good manager who understands the game—sees something maybe more important to the kingdom. He sees the sacrifice. He sees the poor widow dropping in her two copper coins, doing what she can to advance the runners. She won't end up on the big memorial plaque in the fellowship hall, she won't have a room named after her, she won't get to stand at first base, but she's laid down the perfect bunt, and for the little things she's done, the runners have advanced.

And if there is anything that Jesus seems concerned about when he has his debates with the religious leaders, it's "Are we advancing the runners? Are we finding our own good in the good of the whole? Have we made it less about us and more about them?" You can hit three home runs to the applause of the crowd, but if the team loses, the team loses. And if the team loses, you lose.

My kingdom for a bunt, Jesus says. Have you advanced the runners? Have you sacrificed your at-bat to make sure that you've put others in a good position? Have you used your time on the stage well by giving yourself to a cause greater than yourself?

The great Willie Mays entered baseball soon on the heels of Jackie Robinson while segregation remained largely the de facto law of the land. He was signed by the New York Giants and immediately sent to their minor league team in Trenton, the Trenton Giants, and was the first black player in all of that particular league. He met the team in Hagerstown, Maryland, and when his first professional game was over, the team loaded onto the bus and drove to the colored section of town and dropped Mays, and Mays alone, at a hotel there on the other side of the tracks. The rest of the team went across town to the whites-only hotel. Having played in the Negro Leagues up until then, Mays knew team segregation, but not individual segregation. There he sat, a young kid far from home, all alone. Strange place, strange town. At midnight there came a knock on his hotel window. It was three of his Giants teammates who had scaled the fire escape. They wanted to check on him. Mays insisted he was all right. But they insisted that they were spending the night. The three slept on the floor, got up at 6 a.m., returned to their hotel, and saw Mays later in the afternoon when the bus picked him up. They didn't mention it, but Mays knew by their visit that the team was the team and the team protects its own. Sacrifice bunt, runners advance.

Richard Hoffer in his great essay on Mickey Mantle wrote about how Mickey always swung from the heels—in other words, swung for the fences. "The world," Hoffer writes, "will always belong to those who swing from the heels." And so it is. But what about the kingdom of God? My kingdom, Jesus says, for a good sacrifice bunt. My kingdom for two copper coins. My kingdom for those willing to advance the runners. Many attend, but few understand.

I'll never forget a story told me by a dear friend. He was an actor, and he left the Broadway stage to try his hand in Hollywood. It took him a few months of auditions and callbacks to get his first part in a big Hollywood movie. It was a movie starring Tom Hanks—perhaps the largest box-office draw of our time. Not only was he in the same movie as Tom Hanks, he even had a scene with Tom Hanks that included dialogue with him. Often when making movies, when a big actor like Tom Hanks is in a dialogue with a minor character, they shoot the big actor's part of the dialogue and then let him go back to his trailer and they put a stand-in for him to shoot the other part of the dialogue with the bit actor, which was my friend. However, in this scene, Tom Hanks noticed my friend's anxiety over being in his first movie and realized what it might mean if instead of heading back to his trailer he would stay on the set and shoot the scene with my friend and work him through his part. Coach him. Feed him his lines. Encourage him. Advance the runner. In the grand scheme of Hollywood it wasn't a big deal, a small part for a celluloid giant, but to my friend it was the world. A bunt never forgotten. Runner advanced. Many attend, few understand.

I am reminded of a time years ago when, as a pastor, I had to take an unpopular stand on a matter in the church that left me quite open for criticism. Folks disagreed. Folks were disappointed. Folks didn't really care to hear my side of the story. No fun when they are booing from the stands. No fun when the hate mail gets delivered. But people are people, and that's what people, even church people, sometimes do. But it got to the point that I didn't want to go to the mailbox or answer the phone. So another pile of letters was placed on my desk, and there was one I was waiting for—a letter from a person clearly on the other side, a good friend whom I knew was in great disagreement with me. I cringed as I opened the envelope and braced myself for the invective. "Dear Steve," he wrote, "I don't agree with you, but I believe in you. We'll get through this." That's all he wrote. Just a few words. A soft bunt down the third-base line. A small sacrifice of his own ego and his need to be right. The runner was advanced. And he was right: we somehow got through it.

William F. Buckley relayed the story that took place during the fateful events around the rescue at Dunkirk during the throes of World War II—the anxious flight of Allied citizens and soldiers after their defeat at Dunkirk. Ground personnel, Red Cross workers, and embassy staff were all forced to the coast awaiting rescue from the British government. Every imaginable and available ship, including the old ocean liner the *Lancastria*, was sent to rescue as many as possible. Once they filled the old *Lancastria* and pulled up anchor and began their course to Britain, a German bomber dropped a shell into the funnel of the ship and blew a huge hole in the side. The ship immediately took on a terrible list. In the hold were several hundred soldiers trapped with no chance of getting out. While the rest of the passengers and crew were bailing and being rescued by lifeboats, a Roman Catholic priest, a chaplain, donning a Royal Air Force uniform, got himself a rope and managed to lower himself into the hold of the ship, into the gathering of those desperate men, knowing that there would be no chance of getting out. So down he went.

When the survivors of the *Lancastria* made it to Britain and began to tell their stories of the ordeal—the panic and fear while being rescued from the sinking ship—many recounted how close they came to losing hope, but the only thing that kept them going was listening to the singing—those trapped soldiers singing hymns. Led by the priest, of course. Encouraged in their last moments. The last two coins given. Runners advanced.

My kingdom, says Jesus, for a bunt.

CHAPTER 26

Missing Pieces

Romans 3:21–26; 1 Timothy 1:12–17

For a week every year the McConnell clan descends on a beach house on the North Carolina coast—at least three generations of us—to spend a few days reconnecting as family, telling the same stories, laughing at the same jokes, and learning about what life has brought us over the past twelve months. One of the family this year brought a jigsaw puzzle. Not a big one, five hundred pieces, but enough to occupy the lulls of time and the bad-weather afternoons you invariably get at the beach. I'm not a puzzle person, but I watched over the days as different family members tried their hand at assembling it, and gradually the puzzle took shape, until the next to the last day. On that day just a few pieces remained. Easily they fit into their spaces until it became apparent that we were one piece short. We looked here and there and everywhere for the one piece. Nowhere to be found. Strangely its place in the puzzle was smack dab in the middle. You could not look at the beautiful picture that the puzzle had created without noticing the big blank spot right in the middle. We committed a half hour to looking for the missing piece, and we could not find it. So close—one piece away—but so far. The only thing you could see after those days of puzzle assembly was the missing piece. And for the owner of the puzzle at least, the one who had worked the hardest on it, it was a little hard to let go. Four hundred ninety-nine pieces, and all you have is the reminder that it is not complete. (The good news is that the following day we found it right underneath the table, its colors blending in with the color of the rug. It made a couple of people very happy.)

But usually the story doesn't end that way, does it? Your story. My story. We have an idea of how the puzzle is supposed to look and where all the pieces are supposed to go—but life is seldom a completed puzzle. As hard as we try, there always seem to be a few pieces missing. As much as we want to have our acts together, as much as we want to be batting 1.000, as much as we would like to record a perfect score, life doesn't work that way.

Chad Harbach, in his compelling novel *The Art of Fielding*, tells the story of a college baseball player, Henry Skrimshander. Henry plays shortstop for his college team, and he dedicates his life to becoming a great baseball player. He's good at the bat, but he's even better in the field. In fact, he runs up a streak of errorless games that threatens the all-time record of errorless games played by any player—an amazing feat by a shortstop, who gets plenty of opportunities to boot the ball. Henry eats and sleeps baseball, outpracticing his teammates hours each day so that he can become the best.

Harbach describes Henry's philosophy this way:

> Baseball was an art, but to excel at it you had to become a machine. It didn't matter how beautifully you performed SOMETIMES [emphasis in original], what you did on your best day, how many spectacular plays you made. You weren't a painter or a writer—you didn't work in private and discard your mistakes, and it wasn't just your masterpieces that counted. What mattered, as for any machine, was repeatability. Moments of inspiration were nothing compared to elimination of error. . . . Can you make that throw one hundred times out of a hundred? If it can't be a hundred, it had better be ninety-nine.

Well, just as he is a game shy of breaking the record—just as he is prepared to enter the annals of immortality—Henry gets a ground ball, and he throws the ball wildly to first base, missing the first baseman and beaning a fellow player in the dugout in the head, nearly killing him. Henry is completely undone by this. And from that point on, the nearly perfect fielder can't bring himself to field any ball. The balls that are hit to him he can hardly catch, and those balls he catches he can hardly throw. He can't let go of the missing piece, and he ends up quitting the team.

Life has a lot to do with how you handle the missing pieces.

Maybe that's why many of us like baseball so much. Baseball is filled with missing pieces. When you are up to bat in baseball, you must face the prospect that you will fail more than you succeed. The greatest hitting percentage for a season in professional baseball—.406—was recorded by the great Red Sox hitter Ted Williams in 1941. For every ten times he batted, he hit safely four times. Six outs to every four hits. There was a greater chance of Williams making an out than hitting safely, and that was his greatest of seasons. For his career he batted .344, a Hall of Fame percentage. Nearly twice as many outs as hits over his career, and that is arguably the best hitter ever in the game! No other game absorbs as much failure as baseball. Perhaps the greatest and most unbeatable record in the game—if not all sports—is Joe DiMaggio's fifty-six-game hitting streak. Fifty-six games in a row with at least one hit, a record that some think will never be matched. Yet even during that streak, DiMaggio recorded more outs than hits. The best hitter for the Tampa Bay Rays, James Loney, hits safely less than one-third of the time.

"No one," said Lou Brock, a Hall of Fame player, "can ever master the game of baseball or conquer it. You can only challenge it."

Life has a lot to do with how you handle the missing pieces.

I suppose that is what the apostle Paul was getting at in his letter to the Romans. Seeking to understand and explain the human condition, he says it plainly and succinctly: "All have sinned and fallen short of the glory of God." In other words, none of us are able to master the game. Paul, in the selection from 1 Timothy, gets personal and says about himself, "Even though I was formerly a blasphemer, a persecutor, and a man of violence I received mercy. The saying is sure and worthy of full acceptance, that Christ Jesus came into the world to save sinners—of whom I am the foremost." No person understood the human condition more than Paul, and the human condition is that human beings are a mess. They get it wrong more than they get it right. Paul knew that because he saw it mostly in himself, and he didn't have self-help books for support. No matter how much you practice, no matter how many times you've been around the block, no matter how many hours you've studied, no matter how many symbols you have of success—the truth is that we're still a mess, because we can't help ourselves. Three out of ten for you and me is a good life. We may have a few pieces in the right place, but we have more gaps than pieces. If the apostle were to walk into Barnes and Noble and pick up *30 Days to a New You*, he would start to laugh. Thirty days? New you? Self-help? Oh no, says Paul, oh no—it is in Christ that I am a new creation. The past is finished and gone; everything has become new. We live by grace. We live with the profound understanding that we cannot master the game. We cannot conquer the game. We can only challenge the game. We live by grace.

The greatest step we can take in our lives, of course, is when we can see ourselves for who we really are, when we can look in the mirror and both cry and laugh, when we can take ourselves both seriously and lightly enough to see that we are never going to get anywhere on our own merits.

It makes me think of players like Mark McGwire, Barry Bonds, and Alex Rodriguez. In their time they were some of the highest-paid players in baseball, and now they perhaps are the most vilified—mocked, shamed, and booed now more than they are ever applauded. And while each had his own road toward vilification, the truth is that they could not play to their contracts. No one could play to contracts like theirs. They demand perfection. They demand performance-enhancing drugs. They demand a hit every time! But all have sinned. All fall short of the glory. And anyone who places themselves in the position of aiming for perfection loses the point. The box doesn't have enough pieces. The picture will never be perfect.

"Perfectionism," says Anne Lamott, "is based on the obsessive belief that if you run carefully enough, hitting each stepping-stone just right, you won't have to die. The truth is that you will die anyway and that a lot of people who aren't even looking at their feet are going to do a whole lot better than you, and have a lot more fun while they are doing it."

Can you claim your imperfection?

Paul Tournier, the great Swiss twentieth-century Christian psychologist, was once giving a lecture in the United States about the Christian life. At the end of the lecture a young man got up and starting railing about how the problem with the church is that it is filled with hypocrites. And he went on and on about how so many Christians are hypocrites. But Dr. Tournier, who spoke French, did not understand what the young man meant by the word, "hypocrite." Finally someone explained to Tournier what the word meant—someone who says one thing and does another. And Dr. Tournier, finally understanding the word's definition, said, "Ah, c'est moi! C'est moi!"

"I received mercy," Paul writes to Timothy, "so that in me, as the foremost of the sinners, Jesus Christ might display the utmost patience, making me an example to those who would come to believe in him for eternal life." The utmost patience. This is the God who watches us from the stands, the One of the utmost patience. He sees the missing pieces. He sees the strikeouts. He sees the dribbles hit back to the mound. He sees the wild throws. He sees us tripping over our own laces. But he is utmost patient. He knows the game. We cannot master it. We cannot conquer it. We can only challenge it. And he will claim us even still.

Think of even the great twentieth-century prophet Dietrich Bonhoeffer, who was martyred by the Nazis during the closing days of World War II. It's hard to find a church leader like Bonhoeffer, whose life was such a profound example of faithful obedience. And yet when left alone to his thoughts in that Nazi prison searching his soul, he doubted his own authenticity and despaired over his own duplicitous nature. He was strong on the outside but weak on the inside. He wrote a poem, too long to quote in its entirety, but the poem ends as follows:

> Who am I? This man or that other?
> Am I then this man today and tomorrow another?
> Am I both all at once? An imposter to others,
> But to me little more than a whining, despicable
>   weakling?
> Does what is in me compare to a vanquished army,
> That flees in disorder before a battle already won?

Who am I? They mock me these lonely questions of mine.
Whoever I am, you know me, O God. You know I am yours.

You know I am yours.

I am yours. Despite the missing pieces, the .300 average, the hypocrisy, I am yours.

Years ago I had a conversation with a friend of mine about recurring dreams. Many of us have recurring dreams. Mine is the dream of waking up late for a test without having studied—and the excruciating run to the classroom to take a test for which I am not only late but also unprepared. My friend shared with me his own recurring dream—that he is on the pitcher's mound in a professional baseball game and every pitch is slammed for a home run. He is getting killed on the mound, and the fans are booing and he has this feeling of hopelessness. He looks over at the dugout and sees the manager coming out to the mound. In baseball, when the manager walks to the mound it means you are coming out, you're done. So the manager ascends the mound, and my friend looks at him: it's the face of his father. His dad says to him, "It's okay, Son. You're going to be all right." And that's how his dream always ends. "It's okay, Son. You're going to be all right."

"All have sinned and fallen short of the glory of God." It's the secret of the saints, isn't it? The art of the game is to know that. Whoever I am, O God, you know I am yours. Despite who we are, despite what we've done, despite how many selves there are inside and outside, despite how many swings and misses and wild throws to first—God's patience is utmost. His grace is sufficient. He knows the game is never mastered, never conquered, just challenged. Three hits out of ten, and that's all right.

Missing pieces, but he still sees the picture. Whoever I am, O God, I am yours. Always yours.

CHAPTER 27

The Spirit of the Law

Luke 15:11–32; 1 Corinthians 9:19–23

A FEW YEARS AGO THE baseball world was met with a moment of heartache. Armando Galarraga was pitching for the Detroit Tigers up in Detroit against the Cleveland Indians. Galarraga was on his way to pitching a perfect game. A perfect game in baseball is when no batter from the opposing team makes it to first base safely. Twenty-seven hitters up and 27 hitters down. It is a rare moment in baseball. Only twenty-three times in 133 years has a perfect game been pitched. No hits, no walks, no errors. Armando Galarraga had faced twenty-six batters and, as they say in baseball, retired them all. Only one left.

At first base was umpire Jim Joyce, a highly respected umpire with years and years of exceptional work calling balls and strikes, safes and outs. Jason Donald was the twenty-seventh hitter of the night, and he struck a ground ball to the second-base side of the field, which many assumed would be the last out of the game. The ball went deep into the hole, making it a less-than-routine play. But Miguel Cabrera got the ball to the first baseman in time, by at least a half-step before the runner. In the eyes of most witnessing the event, it was the culminating out of a perfect game. Everybody saw it. Everybody knew, everybody except Jim Joyce. But Jim Joyce was the umpire and what Jim Joyce saw was the runner arrive before the ball. Out went his arms. Safe. The Tigers were stunned. The fans were stunned. Manager Jim Leyland was stunned. Armando Galarraga was stunned. A perfect game illegitimately denied. They argued. They begged for the call to be overturned. They looked at the video for proof, and proof was there. They appealed to the commissioner. Can't something be done to grant this pitcher what was his due? No. The rule is the rule. Jim Joyce knew he had made the wrong call. He apologized to the denied pitcher. But once the umpire makes his call, the call stands. Right or wrong. That's the law.

The results, though, were heartbreaking.

Baseball, like any other sport—or any other game for that matter—maintains itself by virtue of its rules, its laws. The laws are there to make things fair—to prevent any player, any team, from gaining an unfair advantage. Competition remains compelling only with some assurance that the rules are the same for everybody. The steroid scandal in baseball has left a pall on the game because it calls into question how level the playing field has been or is, even now. No player or team should be left at a disadvantage. It's one thing to feel the pain of losing within the fairness of competition, but it is more than heartbreaking when the law itself puts someone at a disadvantage. Armando

Galarraga did everything he was required to do to be listed in the history books, but the law said otherwise.

Any game, society, or culture has to wrestle with the unintended consequences of the law. Certainly our good country has wrestled throughout its history with the intended or unintended consequences of the law. Jim Crow laws were present in many states for a long time, but the law itself was the problem and hearts and lives were broken as a result. Even today the debate over voting rights and immigration and marriage are struggles to understand how the law should read and be enforced to give everyone the fairest of advantages.

Certainly the law was at the center of Jesus' teaching and ministry. What to do when the law, instead of drawing people to God, pushes them away? What to do when the law places some in a position of advantage and privilege and others at a disadvantage? What to do when the law—intended to provide people a discipline and ritual of life whereby they might experience a deeper communion with God—is all of a sudden turned around to be used as a gate, and sometimes a weapon, against those whose lives made it difficult to achieve such discipline and ritual? Jesus was seeing this situation as the norm of religious life in his day; the law was creating an unlevel playing field. Some were clearly at a disadvantage.

Scripture tells us that the good rabbi took his place not among the law abiders but among the lawbreakers. "Tax collectors and sinners" is what Luke calls them. They were coming near to hear him. They were brushing up against him. Too close for comfort for the umpires—the Pharisees—who thought they were calling the play. "He hangs out," they said, "with the unclean ones, the sinners, the tax collectors, the disadvantaged, the ones not playing by the rules."

"What's the point of the rules?" Jesus asked. And so he tells some stories, the most famous of which is the story of the father with two sons. Like any father with two sons there are rules. Every child needs rules. The older son is the one who's decided to play by the rules, and the younger son has chosen not to. He goes outside the rules. He goes outside the family farm. He goes to the far country to make up his own rules. And when he realizes how far he has taken himself away from the ritual and routine of life with his father, he turns to go home. When he arrives, he is the first to say that he has broken the rules—but for the grateful father the rules are beside the point. Time to kill the fatted calf, time to strike up the band. My son was lost and is now found, was dead and is now alive.

But then there is that elder son who says, "What about the rules? Don't we have rules anymore? Don't we care about the rules?" The father answers, "Son, you're missing the point. The rules are about us. They are about family. They are about the joy of home, the ritual of relationships. It would break my heart if the rules kept your brother from the joy of home."

"Oh, no," says the umpire, Pharisee, older brother. "Oh no, we have rules, and rules are rules."

And Jesus says, "The family was not made for the rules, son. The rules were made for the family."

Do you recall a few years ago a women's college softball game played between Central Washington and Western

Oregon? The two teams competed hard for the conference championship that year. They were in the second game of a doubleheader when Western Oregon star Sara Tucholsky came to the plate. She was a good hitter but had never before hit a home run. Then came her moment. With two on, she hit one over the fence. In her excitement, though, as she rounded first base, she forgot to touch the bag. The rules say you have to touch the bag. As soon as she went past she remembered, so she turned around to go back and touch first. But as she turned, her leg did not pivot correctly, and before she knew it her knee gave way and she went to the ground with what would later be found to be a torn ACL. In great pain and unable to stand, she crawled back to first base. What to do? The manager asked the umpire, What can we do? She hit a home run, but she can't round the bases. The rules say that if any of her own teammates help her, she will be called out. If they replace her with a runner, she can only be granted first base because she herself did not round the bases. What to do?

That's when Mallory Holtman from Central Washington—the other team—who held the record for the most home runs in the conference, stepped forward to offer that nothing in the rules said that players from the opposing team couldn't help her, couldn't carry her, couldn't make sure that she got what she deserved. No, said the umpire, nothing in the rules said that the other team couldn't help. So Mallory and another teammate picked up their opponent and walked her around the diamond, leaning over to touch her foot on the bases and bringing her home for what would become the winning run of the game.

There is, you see, the letter of the law and the spirit of the law.

It explains, doesn't it, why the apostle wrote to those Corinthians—who seemed pretty torn up about who's following the rules and who's not following the rules, who's keeping the law and who's not. And it seems that they are missing the point. Paul says, "To the Jews I became a Jew, in order to win Jews. To those under the law I became as one under the law so that I might win those under the law. To those outside the law I became as one outside the law so that I might win those outside the law. To the weak, I became weak, so that I might win the weak. I have become all things to all people, that I might by all means save some."

It is the spirit of the law, Paul says. It's the purpose of God that all might be drawn into the irresistible grace. The law serves us no good if the law should prevent us from welcoming all into the kingdom of God.

You likely have heard the apocryphal story of the two American GIs in Normandy during World War II who carried their dead comrade to be buried in a cemetery. They found a cemetery and went to the rectory and asked permission of the Roman Catholic priest to bury him inside the walls of this Catholic cemetery, and the priest said, "Well, you know the rule is that you've got to be Roman Catholic; you've got to be a member of the parish. So I'm sorry. I don't think I can. The rules won't allow it."

The two comrades implored him to change his mind. "It's wartime. Can't you make an exception? It would mean so much."

"I'm so sorry," the priest said. "The rules are the rules. You are welcome, though, to bury him outside the fence, just anywhere outside the fence."

The two GIs reluctantly dug the grave, said a prayer, and buried their comrade. They planned to return the next day to put a marker at the grave.

So the next afternoon they returned and went to the part along the fence where they dug their grave, but they couldn't find it. No grave. They walked all up and down the fence, and they couldn't find where they'd dug the grave! They knew they'd dug it. They walked all around the cemetery, all around that fence, and they couldn't find it.

Finally they went in to see the priest and said, "Father, forgive us. We were the ones who came yesterday."

He said, "Oh, yes. I remember."

They said, "Forgive us for bothering you, but we asked for permission to bury our comrade inside the fence, and you said, 'Bury him outside,' and we did, but we can't find it. Are we lost? Where is the grave we dug? Do you know what might have happened to it?"

The priest said, "Oh, yes. I know what happened. I was so upset about your visit yesterday that I spent half the night worrying about what I said to you. And I spent the other half of the night moving the fence."

There is the law, and then there is the spirit of the law.

A couple of decades ago, another heartbreaking moment flashed before us from the diamond. Hall of Fame second baseman Roberto Alomar, playing for Baltimore, was called out on a third strike by another one of the game's great umpires, John Hirschbeck. It was a bad call, and it brought the two men face-to-face in a verbal battle that we are used to seeing in baseball. But this time something terrible happened. Roberto Alomar—known around the league as being one of the more respectful of players—lost his mind for a moment and did the unthinkable: he spit into the umpire's face. It was in the baseball world or any world the worst he could have done, and it turned the entire baseball world against the star player. It went downhill from there, and the two men became the bitterest of enemies. Hirschbeck carried a grudge against the second baseman for years, but the rules were the rules and there was no obligation on the rule keeper's part to show a shred of grace.

But then one day when Hirschbeck was preparing to umpire another game with Robbie Alomar at second base, he asked a veteran attendant what he thought about Alomar. The man replied, "He is one of the two nicest men in baseball."

"Oh yeah?" replied the umpire. "And who's the other?"

"You," the man said.

And that was the moment when the rules no longer mattered. The next day Hirschbeck was the second-base umpire just behind Roberto Alomar. "Hey, Robbie," said the umpire, "how you doing?" And with that the floodgates opened, and the spirit of the law began to blow. The next day Hirschbeck asked Alomar to come see his family. And the two have since become friends. When Alomar was voted into the Hall of Fame, Hirschbeck said he was the greatest second baseman he'd ever seen play the game.

"To those under the law I became as one under the law so that I might win those under the law. To those outside the law I became as one outside the law so that I might win those outside the law. To the weak I became weak so that I might win the weak."

And, yes, there is an end to that heartbreaking story of the umpire and the pitcher and the lost perfect game. Umpire Jim Joyce was on rotation the next day to umpire behind home plate, and baseball officials said it would be all right if he took a pass and sat out the game out of fear of how the fans would treat him. No, said Joyce, I need to face the music. So as he stepped out of the tunnel, he heard something he wasn't expecting to hear. He heard cheers. A couple of boos, but mostly cheers. Applause from the crowd. Word had gotten out about the umpire's remorse. Before the game, the customary meeting of the managers takes place at home plate so that the teams can exchange lineup cards. Umpire Jim Joyce called for the managers to come forward, but out of the Detroit dugout came, not the manager, but the pitcher of the night before, Armando Galarraga. He came to shake the umpire's hand. He came to say it was all right.

"How could you do that?" the reporters asked the pitcher after the game. "How could you so graciously extend yourself to someone who took your perfect game away?"

The pitcher replied, "Perfect? Nobody's perfect."

CHAPTER 28

Safe at Home

—~—

Ecclesiastes 3:1–15

It happens every late August. The highways are jammed with them. Travel down any interstate and you'll see station wagons, SUVs, and trailers filled with stuff—college stuff—purchased recently at Bed, Bath and Beyond and Target and Walmart. Somewhere in the midst of the stuff is a college freshman making the journey to the school of his or her choice. Leaving home after eighteen years of preparation, learning to talk and walk and take out the trash and wash the dishes and say please and clean your room and algebra and Spanish and field hockey and soccer. Now it is time to leave home, to leave the nest. It takes a bird about fourteen days to leave the nest. It takes an American kid eighteen years, and we think we are the most intelligent of the species. It's not that they don't come back. They do. Sometimes in weeks. Sometimes for Thanksgiving. Sometimes for summer. Sometimes for years!

But it's never quite the same. Once you leave home, you leave home.

You remember leaving home, don't you? Maybe it was to college, maybe it was to a job. Maybe it was to get married. Maybe it was simply to live on your own. But you left home. It's what we are supposed to do. Wings expand and we flutter to another tree. We are on our own to fend for ourselves, to make our own way, to figure it out. Leaving home is part of the human journey.

It is, as well, the point of the game of baseball: to leave home. It's what a batter wants to do. Get a hit. Make his way to the bases. Leaving home is what the pitcher doesn't want you to do. He wants you out—out on strikes, out at first, but out. Still, the purpose of the game is to leave home, because you have to leave home before you can go home. In baseball it is all about home, getting around the bases and home safely.

Easier said than done. It's hard to get home safely. A hit is very little guarantee that you will arrive home safely. Making it to first is hard enough, but getting from first to home is a whole other thing. Lots of things have to happen if you are going to arrive home safely in baseball. Getting on base is just the first step. All sorts of peril lie in wait for you on the bases. You can get picked off. You can get caught stealing. You can be the front end of a double play. You can languish while your teammates fail to bat you in. You can get caught in a pickle. All sorts of things can happen to you on the bases and can make your going home a very difficult thing to do. There is a statistic in baseball called "left on base." These are those who left home and never got home.

Lots of things can happen between leaving home and getting home.

It is, I think, what the writer of Ecclesiastes was concerned with when he wrote his little piece of wisdom literature. Not baseball, of course, but the fortunes and misfortunes that lie between leaving home and going home. Lots happens in the interim. "For everything there is a season, and a time for every matter under heaven," he writes. "A time to be born, and a time to die; a time to plant, and a time to pluck up what is planted; a time to kill and a time to heal; a time to break down, and a time to build up," and on and on it goes. The yin and the yang of life. "A time to seek, and a time to lose; a time to keep, and a time to throw away." Life is filled with its seasons. It won't always be good, and it won't always be bad. Sometimes you're out, and sometimes you're safe.

Life—once we leave home—doesn't always give us what we want.

In the movie *Field of Dreams* is a character named Doc Graham. He's been a doctor in a little town up in Minnesota for fifty years. He's taken care of bumps and bruises, coughs and mumps for fifty years, quietly loved and respected by his whole town. But he carries inside him the small ache of not achieving a childhood dream—to get a chance to take an at-bat in a major league baseball game. He came close by playing half an inning in the field, but he never got to the plate. And he always wondered what it would have been like to face a major league pitcher and to tell about it the rest of your life. Ray Kinsella exclaims, "Fifty years ago, for five minutes you came within . . . y-you came this close. It would KILL some men to get so close to their dream and not touch it. God, they'd consider it a tragedy." To which the good doctor replies, "Son, if I'd only gotten to be a doctor for five minutes, now that would've been a tragedy."

Life does not always give us our dreams. We have our seasons. There is a time to keep and a time to lose.

It's what I love about the season of baseball. No sport has a longer season. Six months, not counting the playoffs and World Series. Six months. A lot can happen in six months. One hundred sixty-two games. Twice as many as basketball and hockey, and ten times as many as football. A lot can happen in a season of six months and 162 games. Slumps and streaks. Injuries and recoveries. Trades and sales. A hitter who has a four-strikeout game does not define the entire season by one game. News of a player out for a month with an injury is not the end of the world. The baseball season allows for many seasons. It allows for the ups and downs, the good and the bad. You don't get measured by the game or by the at-bat or by the pitch; you get measured by the season. The long season. How well did you do over the season? How consistent were you over the season? It's what divides a fan from a manager. A fan views baseball one game at a time. What have you done for me lately? So-and-so is a bum because he struck out in the bottom of the ninth. But a manager looks at the season, the season of seasons. The ups and the downs. The streaks and the slumps. The injuries and the recoveries. How well did you do over the season? Because, like running the bases, the season is filled with perils. Bad things can happen. Unexpected things can happen. Miracles can happen. Luck can happen. Fortune can happen. And it's hard to make sense of it all. It's what the great teacher in Ecclesiastes would want to tell us. Bad things happen to good people. Good things happen to bad people. There are no guarantees once you leave home.

Bob Seger—the great Motor City rocker and part-time theologian—wrote a song I heard a thousand times while growing up called "Hollywood Nights." It's a song about a midwestern boy who is tired of living at home and he wants to go find himself out west: "see some old friends, good for the soul." He ends up in Los Angeles and before long finds himself charmed by the big-city lights and the high rolling hills and the attractiveness of a certain young woman. All of it exerts its seductive power on the young man to the point, Seger says, that he knew "he was too far from home." The boy gives in to it all and lives the high life for a time until one morning he wakes up alone. The air is out of the balloon, like the prodigal son waking up in the pig sty—all alone feeding pigs and wanting to eat the pods. Now the boy wonders if he can ever go back home.

This slump in my life—will it keep me from home? That is the existential question. Can we ever get back home? Can you ever get too far from home?

It's been almost three thousand years since Homer wrote his epic poem, *The Odyssey*. But it's a story we keep on telling, because it is a story about going home. Returning from the

Trojan war, Odysseus must make his way home, and home is not easy to get to. He must face the monsters and the temptresses and the forces of nature. It's hard to get home. Sometimes the wind is at your back and sometimes the wind is against you, but always the journey is to go home. Bart Giamatti, the great former commissioner of baseball, whose tenure was cut short at a young age from a heart attack, reminded us, "All literary romance derives from the *Odyssey* and is about rejoining—rejoining a beloved, rejoining parent to child, rejoining a land to its rightful owner or rule. Romance is about putting things aright after some tragedy has put them asunder. It is about restoration of the right relationship among things—and going home is where the restoration occurs because that is where it matters most." Giamatti said that's what baseball is all about—going home.

Home is what matters most.

The great narrative of life, the great narrative of scripture, is about you and me trying to find our way home. We go from creation to cross to resurrection. "Our hearts are restless," Augustine wrote, "until they find their rest in thee." Life is about leaving home and going home. And we want to go home because home is where we are rejoined. Home is where we find ourselves. Home is where we are finally reconciled to the God who has loved us all along, the one with whom we are seeking reunion. "Our commonwealth is in heaven," wrote the apostle.

We leave home to go home.

It makes me think of Robert Frost's great poem "The Death of the Hired Man," about a farmhand who keeps leaving the farmstead and returns from season to season—to the great frustration of the farmer, who wants him to stay. He's unreliable. But now he has come back, and he is not in good health. But the farmer's had it. He doesn't want him back. But his wife appeals for the hired man. "Warren," she says, "he has come home to die. You needn't be afraid he'll leave you this time."

"Home," he mocked gently. "It all depends on what you mean by home. . . . Home is the place where, when you have to go there, they have to take you in."

To which she replies, "I should have called it something you somehow haven't to deserve."

Something you haven't to deserve.

And that is the good news for you and me, isn't it? That amid the seasons of life—the perils of the bases, the ups and the downs, the times to weep and to laugh, the times to hate and to love, the times to seek and to lose, the times to sew and to tear, the times when we slide safely and the times when we are thrown out—none of us gets it right all the time. At best we bat .300. But home is where we are headed. Home is something we haven't to deserve. We are saved by grace, not by works. We are in the long season. The journey. The odyssey. The way back home.

"Be sure," wrote C. S. Lewis, "that the ins and the outs of your individuality are no mystery to God; and one day they will be no mystery to you. The mold in which a key is made would be a strange thing, if you had never seen a key; and the key itself a strange thing if you had never seen a lock. Your soul has a curious shape because it is a hollow made to fit a particular swelling in the infinite contours of the divine substance, or a key to unlock one of the doors in the house with many mansions."

Or as John Newton, the old, wicked slave trader and repentant believer, the one who understood about the seasons of life, wrote in his great hymn,

> Through many dangers, toils and snares,
> I have already come.
> Tis grace has brought me safe thus far,
> And grace will lead me home.

We leave home to go home.